T0115038

TODAY'S TOP STORY

is a Four-Letter Word

Reported by
thirty-year veteran TV news reporter, producer, and writer

GERI HEARNE

and cocreated with Spirit

BALBOA
PRESS

A DIVISION OF HAY HOUSE

Joy Media

Joy Media, LLC, is found on the Internet at www.joymediaonline.com.
Joy Media, LLC, sponsors www.heavencantwait.org to help bridge heaven and earth.

All glory goes to God.
Glory to God in the highest. Through Him/Her all things are possible.

Balboa Press books may be ordered through booksellers or by contacting:
Balboa Press
A Division of Hay House
1663 Liberty Drive
Bloomington, IN 47403
www.balboapress.com
1 (877) 407-4847

Printed in the United States of America.

ISBN: 978-1-4525-9575-7 (sc)
ISBN: 978-1-4525-9577-1 (hc)
ISBN: 978-1-4525-9576-4 (e)

Library of Congress Control Number: 2014906435

Balboa Press rev. date: 7/16/2014

This book is dedicated to the people who work as news communicators in television, radio, newspapers, and other printed material and those who publish on the web. It is further dedicated to the people they serve.

All glory to God in the highest.

A good newspaper is a nation talking to itself.
—Arthur Miller

A good book is an author talking to herself.
—Geri Hearne

I'll cut to the chase. Here's my lead: today's top story is a four-letter word. That word is *love*. No matter what your condition is right in this moment regarding your family, your home, your career, your health, your finances, or even your romantic life, the top story is this: unconditional love is available to you right now, in this moment, and always. You can veer off course, but at any time, you can get back to love, no matter what is going on in your life.

So you don't have to read this book to find out what today's top story is, but if you want to feel what it is and know it experientially, you should continue reading. This book is cocreated with Spirit. Spirit is love, and you can feel it now.

I spent a long time listening to the loving voice inside and around me. I used my basic reporting, writing, and producing skills to question, interpret, and present the material Spirit communicated to me. This book represents my effort to use innate and then honed skills to present communications from beyond the third dimension. With Spirit's help, I am taking what is unseen and helping to make it visible to our everyday world.

CONTENTS

Letter from the Author

Dear Reader,

In this time of change, a lot of us ordinary folk are having extraordinary experiences. We are seeing beyond our five senses and opening up to intuition and more consciousness. This book presents some of my experiences and automatic writings from connecting with Spirit.

I began opening up to Spirit in a big way in 2005. At the time, I was producing a TV show for a network-affiliated TV station in Chicago. The segment I was putting together had to do with making a better omelet by putting broccoli and other veggies into the mix. The tease would be if you, our listener, watched this, you would know how to get more vitamins and minerals in your body and presumably feel better. It wasn't the first time I had produced a segment like this, but it would be close to my very last.

Little did I know that food programming was about to explode in the TV world. People were becoming fascinated with culinary pursuits—especially exotic ingredients and entertaining chefs. But I wasn't feeling the food thing. I seemed to be out of sync with the outer world and TV programming, while I was getting in touch with my inner guidance.

Now, back to the fateful day when I asked God for a change in my life. I was still pulling the information together for what I considered to be a boring food segment. I remember I let out a huge sigh. I was tired of what I was doing, and I needed inspiration.

Remember, this was in 2005, before the economic crisis. If I had that job today, I would feel a lot different about it. I had no idea of what was to come or that finding and keeping a good job would be a blessing in today's world. But back then, I allowed myself the luxury of introducing a dialogue with myself about the worthiness of my work life.

The questions I asked would take me places inside myself I didn't know existed. During the journey, I would spend a year off work and mostly in bed because of an illness. At times, I felt that God was sitting down next to me having a heart-to-heart talk with me. Other times, I felt He/She was sitting on top of me, preventing me from going forward. During those times, I felt like I was getting universal downloads of the most loving kind. I had interesting inner sojourns that took me to other dimensions. I wrote them down, perhaps because the experiences were so unusual for me or maybe it was what God wanted me to do: share His/Her Word. Either way, since I came out on the other side of this journey, I have been happier and have felt more joy. And not only that, any time I feel down, I know how to get myself back into the vibration of love.

Now, more on the first questions I asked.

PART I

COMING TO TERMS: GOD IS TALKING TO ME

Chapter One

THE QUEST BEGINS

Ask, and it is given. I learned this is a spiritual truth. I began asking the questions in 2005. I was at my desk in the newsroom. I was wondering when I had last produced this type of food segment for the weekend show. Was it last week? The week before? Did I use a female or a male chef? Did I invite a Latino or African American? Maybe this time I would invite a child chef. Had anybody done that? How would I tell this same story in yet another different way? I couldn't remember what the last hook was, but I needed one for this week. Maybe I was burned out, but I gave myself the opportunity to wonder, *Is this all there is?* I was producing a food segment that did not fill me up. I wondered, *Where will I be fulfilled?*

I sat back from my desk, looked up, and asked, "God, is this all there is? Eating healthier for a better life? Is there more to this 'feeling better' story?" My boredom was getting the best of me. I started to take it personally. I asked myself several questions: Is this how I will top off my career in TV news? Granted, I did not want to go back to covering murder investigations, and producing shows on terror attacks in our country and "shock and awe" military attacks in other countries. I struggled, what did I want to report on? What do I want to produce? What of substance means something to me and possibly others? How can I make a difference?

In my moment of self-reflection, I looked up and noticed the klieg light hanging from the studio ceiling. (My work desk area in the newsroom doubled as a working studio.) If you are not familiar with this type of light, it has barn doors. It was created by a guy named Klieg. Television and newspaper people, we're always putting our names on what we do. We're individualists. But this individual felt helpless and was wondering if there was something more. What was I was missing? I decided I would not put my name on this show under the title "producer," because, at the time, it meant nothing to me. I felt like that Olympic gymnast with the "I am not impressed" face after receiving a second-place award. She was spoofed by everyone from *Saturday Night Live* to the president of the United States. At this moment, I was unimpressed with myself. And even though I worked on the number-one-rated show in the time slot, I did not feel like a winner.

In my exasperation, I talked to the klieg light located high above my head. It appeared like a metaphor for the light. "Is this all there is, God?" I pleaded.

Since I have a healthy fear of the all-powerful one, I quickly softened my tone. "Well, it's OK if this is all there is, if that's what Your plan is. I'm OK with it—really, I am. I'm OK with it personally and OK with it for the viewers. But I have to imagine there must be something more potent than vegetables for breakfast. Aren't my viewers hungry for something more than morning minerals?" I asked.

A few more sighs later, I said, "If this is it, I will do it. But I don't feel any joy here."

I kept asking, "There must be something else you want me to do?"

So, reader, be careful what you ask for. Remember always: ask, and it is given.

Now, some seven or eight years later, I am fulfilling that desire. I am giving my viewers/readers something more than a healthy diet for their bodies. I am providing here some nourishment for the soul.

What God wanted me to do and the job I finally joyfully embraced is the creation of this book. God encouraged me to write it. Mother Mary helped me get through it. And Jesus cheered me along the way. I am spreading His news in *Today's Top Story.*

But it wouldn't come easily. I couldn't just drop my life and be God's puppet. I had questions and concerns. I was on a treadmill of working, sleeping, and paying bills. And six months after the "klieg" incident, I still hadn't made any changes in my life. So what started out as a whisper, a yearning, grew into a louder, more forceful spiritual push.

I stopped producing the morning show and started filling in where needed. One day, when I was producing a 5:00 p.m. broadcast, something happened after I wrote the last story in the show. It's called a "kicker," a short story on something lighthearted. After it was finished, something forceful near my solar plexus pushed me away from the computer. I heard the words in a loud voice: "You do not want to do this anymore." It annoyed me. I knew the voice was right. But I was helpless.

I looked up, and with my hands held out, I responded, "Yes, I know. But what do You want me to do?"

There was silence, and then there would be more silence. Something needed to change, but I was incapable of making the change myself. I needed to stop producing news shows. But I was afraid to stop receiving the income. That was when I got "sick" and was forced to stay away from television newsrooms for one year. There's more detail about that in chapter 5, but first, I want to talk a little bit about talking with God.

Chapter Two

READ MY WORD

Over the course of the following years (2006 to 2007), three words kept coming to me: *"Read My Word."*

I kept thinking about it. *Read My Word.* Who is that talking inside my head? I said it out loud: "Read My Word." What word? Who's word? I saw it in my mind's eye in book form like this:

READ
MY
WORD

I eventually thought of the Bible. It really was not my first choice, but maybe God wants me to read the Bible.

The odd thing was, I thought, if God knew everything, then surely He knew that He was wasting my time. (I am using the pronoun He here because that's how I referred to God. He went along with my image of an old man with a beard wearing a white toga and sitting among the clouds in heaven. Today, I use the pronoun S/He that I created to be more inclusive. To be clear, I don't think God is a woman/man, but I see God as both masculine and feminine. And I want to portray that in my writing.) I had tried for decades but honestly could not make heads or tails out of many of the Bible stories. I am doing a little better now with some help. Please don't think ill of me or cheer me depending on where you stand on the Bible issue. You see, I have an enormous respect for the Good Book, but through my own ignorance, I just didn't get it. The next chapter details my on-again, off-again relationship with the Good Book.

But for now, I took the words literally and became a lector at my church. I thought if I forced myself to deliver the Word, it would deliver me. I would maybe finally understand it. It didn't work out that way. After a year, I retired my pulpit reading. It was just another attempt to understand God that fell short for me at this time.

He was talking to me, but I was not understanding where He was going. I was not trained to hear Him. I left that to Jesus and maybe the church. I was going in a different direction. Eventually, I finally got it. And here it is: God is talking to me and you all the time. God did not stop talking ten thousand or even two thousand years ago. God talks to us every day, even every moment, if we let Him/Her.

But back to the "Read My Word" message. I took it to mean that I should read the Bible. It was something I had tried to do from an early age and never quite grasped its full meaning.

Chapter Three

Geri and the Bible: A Personal History

ere's a little background on my relationship with the Bible and the church. I grew up in Brooklyn, one of nine children in an Irish-Catholic family. I lived across the street from a very large Roman Catholic church. It's called a basilica. When I was young, I went to Mass every day. The church was a huge, beautiful building, just shy in size and stature of a cathedral in New York City. Every day at noon, the bells would ring twelve times. On special occasions, we were treated with songs. The church had an elementary and high school. Those teachers had an enormous positive influence on me.

The quaint picture I paint was not without its angst. I remember thinking how lucky boys were that they could serve on the altar and get closer to Jesus than I could in my pew behind the pillars. Today, I am happy to see girls sharing the same privilege, serving on the altar.

The Basilica of Our Lady of Perpetual Help held a dedication to Mother Mary. Its elementary and high school teachers instructed us in the Bible stories. The nuns were dedicated to their love, Jesus, and I loved listening to their stories. They taught about Noah being instructed by God to build an ark and how Jesus turned water into wine and healed the sick. I enjoyed the parables and the miracles and wondered what it would be like to hear God's voice. I was in awe of those who had had direct experience with All That Is. But I had never read the Bible cover to cover, and that bothered me. A lot.

It wasn't that I didn't try to read the Bible. I did try—over and over and over again. Today, I have more than a dozen versions in my home. And I'm still not done. While shopping today, I picked up a Bible handbook: *365 Days of Bible Verses*. Maybe if I read one story a day, I might finally get the whole picture. I don't think I will ever give up. But here's more on my personal history.

My love of the Bible actually began before I could read. When I was young, my family had a large maroon-and-gold Bible. The pages were lined in gold leaf. That Bible was one of my go-to toys. I turned the pages and looked at the pictures of the saints. The pictures looked like paintings. I was fascinated by them and studied them well, sort of religiously, if you pardon the pun.

When I began to learn how to read in school, I would return home and try to read the Bible stories. I went from *Run, Jane, Run* to long names detailing who begat whom from Adam to Abraham and the House of David. But I couldn't follow the genealogy. My brain wasn't trained, and the names didn't mean anything to me. I forgot them as fast as I read them.

When I got a little older, I was confused by the violence in our great book. I had many questions and few answers. Why would the God of all be so violent? Why would He want us to sacrifice our children for Him? Where's the compassion for us poor human folk? You would think the God of All That Is would be far above advocating brutality. I was so confused.

A little later, I was somewhat comforted when my Catholic teachers told me the book was inspired by God but written by man. And since man is not perfect, could the Bible be? Then, I was told parts of the Bible might have even been rewritten by those who may have wanted to control the masses for their own gain or for the gain of an organization. If that was true, how would I know which parts were written by man and which were the real word of God? I grew more confused. So, for a time, I blocked myself from reading it altogether.

By the time I hit my teens and twenties, I had turned away from the religious world and focused my attention on the "real" world. Enough of this mumbo-jumbo holy stuff! I wanted to feel the nitty-gritty of what the world was really like. If I couldn't figure out what was true in the Bible, I was going to figure out what was true in the material world. So, with great interest, I studied the corporate world and politics. I wondered what role I would play in it.

Chapter Four

GERI'S ROLE IN THE "REAL" WORLD

T he role I would play took me into reporting on and producing shows about global, national, and local events. I would be a TV news reporter and then producer and writer.

Yes, in my late teens and early twenties, I turned away from religion. Enough of this mumbo-jumbo holy stuff (or so I thought). I had had twelve years of Catholic school, and now I wanted to feel the nitty-gritty of what the world was really like. I wanted to know the truth. I couldn't access spiritual truth, so material truth would be my way. Before heading into a career in TV journalism, I spent a summer at the *National Law Journal* and a memorable year at a Japanese bank at the World Trade Center, and I received college degrees from New York City Community College and Long Island University before getting my master's degree in broadcast journalism at the University of Missouri in Columbia, Missouri.

I felt at home in the "Show Me" state. I felt it was a great follow-up to my hard knocks education in one of New York City's boroughs. In Missouri, I began a thirty-year career in TV journalism, helping my colleagues cover the dioxin contamination in the small town of Times Beach for KOMO TV and KBIA Radio. My career included a TV news reporting job in Terre Haute, Indiana, in which I worked as an investigative journalist and fill-in weekend anchor. I worked in television's largest market, with ABC News in New York and ABC Sports working on the summer Olympics in Los Angeles in 1984. I helped out during football games and once made it inside the booth in Washington DC when Howard Cosell, Dan Meredith, and Frank Gifford were at the helm of *Monday Night Football*. I worked for a now defunct news wire service, United Press International, during a political convention in the early 1980s. I remember seeing lots of Kennedys but mostly being starstruck by Gloria Steinem standing a few feet away from me. Whatever legacy feminism will hold in the future, Steinem was one of the first women to tell young ladies they could be or do whatever they wanted.

I spent most of my career in Chicago as a writer and TV news producer. I helped start up three new news shows at WFLD-TV, and later, I produced the weekend morning news shows for WMAQ-TV. During the course of these decades, I never forgot my calling: a search for truth. I wanted to get at the heart of the things that I was writing, producing, and reporting on. I followed news stories with an unwavering curiosity. Then, some twenty-five years into my career, that all changed.

It was the day that I was picked up and dropped onto a new path, or perhaps I wound myself back to my first one: the real truth. I suddenly knew that the real truth wasn't found in the streets of Brooklyn, in a classroom in Columbia, or covering stories in New York City, Washington DC, or Chicago. In fact, the real truth for me wasn't in the media at all. And it wasn't in any book or course I took along my journey. While all those places and the beautiful people I met along the way certainly helped and guided me, they were all outside of me. My real truth, like yours, is an inside job. And my journey began the day I asked those questions looking up at that klieg light in the news studio.

Chapter Five

GOD SPEAKS TO GERI

So church and The Bible weren't doing it for me through most of the last thirty years. But that didn't stop God from letting me know what He wanted. To be fair, I asked for it. I asked for something meaningful. And He gave it to me. After the "klieg" incident and after I was pushed (felt like being sucker-punched) away from the computer, it didn't take long before I was unable even to get up and go to work. I didn't understand what was wrong with me, but I couldn't get out of bed.

Eventually, the doctors diagnosed me with orbital myositis. It's called a fake tumor. I treated it successfully with steroids. But the condition and the treatment caused me to alter my life. It kept me out of work for a whole year. Not only was I out of my TV news job, but I was unable even to watch television. A thirty-second commercial was too much stimulation for me. I couldn't take the sound or the light; I felt almost like the frequency coming out of the machine was killing me. I spent most of those months in bed. I constantly looked on the bright side though: I was blessed many nights to share dinner with my husband and two sons. That was something that rarely happened while I was working full-time. (In fact, I remember thinking how lovely it would be to have dinner with my husband and children every night. That, I thought, was the perfect definition of a rich woman. And I had that while I was "sick.")

The metaphor of the eye injury was not lost on me. I understood immediately that while I was having trouble in the physical world, I knew that the spiritual world was opening up to me in spades. And the communication was constant. That could be why I had to rest most of the day to take it all in.

From the outside, it looked like my world was falling apart: financial trouble and health concerns. Friends and family would ask me, "What's wrong?" Many times, I answered myself, "You should be asking, 'What's right?'" Because although I was not working in the day-to-day world and there were legitimate concerns about the turn my life appeared to be taking, I felt really good in my heart. For the first time in my life, I was "*be*-ing." I was listening. I was feeling. I was experiencing God inside myself.

Even though I was not a good practicing Catholic—despite my stint as a lector—and even though I could not get God through the Bible, His infinite power, grace, and love came to me. God didn't give up. I couldn't get Him through other channels, so He came to me. Source energy came to me. And I felt His closeness. Outside, my material world was falling apart, but inside, I was growing with Spirit.

Chapter Six

WHAT'S LOVE GOT TO DO WITH IT?

That day in 2005, when I asked those questions, I began my inner journey to truth. Since then, I have learned what my truth is. And it is inside me just like your truth is inside you.

My truth is not reporting or recording news events. My real truth is reporting on my spiritual experiences. They are things most of us cannot see with our eyes or hear with our ears. The experiences come through you, and in many cases, they are invisible. This truth is a larger truth than we get in the news or from government sources. Real truth is larger than human life itself. Real truth, for me, unveiled itself inside of me, and I found it to be a four-letter word: *love*. Today's top story is love, unconditional love. And no matter how your life is going financially, health-wise, or in your career, you have access to unconditional love right now.

Yes, it is love that is the big "secret" that makes life better. I am not talking about romantic love, even though that has an important place in our lives. I am talking about the love that is ever present and everywhere. It is right there for the taking if we could just get out of the way and see it, feel it, and be it. Love. It sounds so simple, but what a challenge it has been for me to accept it, first, and then to live it. Today, I no longer define myself by what I've done but by who I am and how I feel. The question I ask myself is: did I love today? If the answer is no, then I sit back and connect to Spirit again. Spirit is love. And when I love, I express Spirit.

What's love got to do with it? Everything. On the level of God, love is all there is. And we can live on that plane any time we choose.

Chapter Seven

COULD I HANDLE
THE TRUTH?

The messages in this book were written down in January of 2010. Since 2007, I had been writing down Spirit messages and feeling an enormous unconditional love in my heart. I shared a monthly inspiration from Spirit on my website www.heavencantwait.org. But in January of 2010, I received three major communications that were more than monthly guidance. These three "downloads," as I like to call them, are in this book. The material is a primer on how to live day to day, every day, in love along with God. These three spiritual downloads have helped me live a more joyful life, no doubt. But it's not enough that they stop with me. So, in love, I share the messages today, publishing them in 2014.

Why did it take me so long to publish them? I created a self-publishing company, Joy Media, for inspirational stories. I took on other authors' projects yet hesitated to put my own work out in the marketplace. The reason was that I thought I wasn't good enough. And I had little faith.

Can you imagine God talking to me? Who do I think I am? Why would He waste His time on me, such an insignificant person?

I have learned over the last few years that no one is insignificant. Not even me! Every person can make a difference in his or her own life and in the lives of others. Each of us could, at the very least, offer a smile to another child of God. I have learned that I am a person worthy of contributing something—and you are too.

Can I handle this truth of who I am—a piece of God? I wasn't always able to say this. I am thankful that I can today. Yes, I can handle the truth of who I am. And you can too. It's our birthright to communicate with God and act according to His/Her guidance.

So, with that in mind, the first group of spiritual messages I am sharing is: "Forty Days and Forty Nights with Spirit." And so it begins with day 1. I attempted to keep the messages 100 percent accurate—using the words that came to me. When I am uncertain about the meaning of the words, I ask questions. And where I have comments, I let you know that with the words "Geri's Note." My dream and my notes are italicized in day 1.

Part II

Forty Days and Forty Nights with Spirit

Chapter One

THE FIRST TWENTY
MESSAGES

Day 1

If you are lost, it does not matter. Go into your heart, and you will find all things. In love, you will find a sign that points you in the right direction.

Geri's Note: After Spirit gave me the first message, I had a dream and recorded it in my journal. The following is lifted from that journal, which serves as an example of how you will be guided on your own path.

Last night, I dreamed I was in a classroom and a new teacher showed up. I was so frustrated because I just got used to doing things the way the last substitute wanted them done. I asked this new teacher what relevance her work had to what we already knew. She assured me it would be fine. I wasn't so sure but felt a little better.

This teacher liked to eat peanuts. She ate them and had them at her desk at the front of the room. (It's interesting to me that our first message begins with a dream about a teacher with peanuts. Some dream interpreters say peanuts in a dream can mean the desire to get at the truth or core of something. That is precisely what we are doing in this book.) When the teacher took the class for a walk, I presumed she was taking us to where there would be more peanuts. I, along with several of my classmates, got separated from the group. One guy decided to stop looking altogether. He reasoned, "I'm lost; I'm staying put and not exerting any effort to find the group." I decided to stay with him. He did magnificent things in this place. I tried to do those things, but each time, I failed. I wasn't allowed (some invisible glass prevented me from participating) to jump in a waterfall pool like he did or to go to a new section of the hotel where he hung out with others.

Then (and this is still the dream) other classmates came back. One of them said he was going to keep trying to find the group. I felt a strong urge from my heart to help this guy. I told him I would go with him. We retraced our steps. We went to a hallway where we had last seen the class together. He was getting ready to climb the stairs, and I planned to follow him. We stopped. Somehow, we both knew it would be difficult. He wrapped climbing cords around my hands. I was scared, and I told him so.

"Scared? Yeah, right." He thought that comment of mine was silly. I think he actually assumed that I was brave. I didn't feel courageous.

I looked down. On the floor, I saw the collar of the teacher's dress. It was one of those collars that snap on a dress. It was black velvet with a few sparkles. The sparkles were facing toward the stairs. It looked like a one-way sign. And in seeing this visual sign, I knew I was going the right way. That was the end of the dream. My interpretation follows.

In life, you will find your way if you act from your heart. You will see signs that point the way. It seems to me that some things in my dream weren't pertinent to my message, but it shows how lost we can become. How many times do I wander, how many times do I want to jump in a waterfall instead of climbing the stairs? These are metaphors for the range of choices we have in life. We are shown many roads, but only a few are ours to follow. You will know which ones to keep pursuing by trying things that don't work so well for you as they do for another.

If you notice, some of our choices are easy and we glide through them; others, we get shut out of. And there are many distractions. We all get lost along the way. One of my classmates in the dream was jumping down waterfalls. How fun was that? I thought. I'd like to do that. But it turned out not to be my way at all. I had to stop and open up to another opportunity because somehow I was prevented from going to the area where the waterfalls were. I had a stronger feeling of wanting to help the other classmate find the group. I embarked on that task. It makes me feel like we all have an inner GPS, and rather than calling it a global positioning system, we could call it our guiding personal system.

In the dream, the moment that I found the visual sign of the sparkles pointing the way for me, I felt both joy and fear. I interpret it this way: when we find the path, we should acknowledge both the joy and fear, because fear comes hand in hand with joy. It is the other side of the coin. So, on this road, when we see our path, we are given at least two gifts. The first one is the gift of guidance to get back on our road to joy after being lost. The second is the divine opportunity to overcome our fear.

Day 2

When you desire something, you don't need to spell it all out. Spirit knows that which you want.

With Spirit, it is not necessary to spell it all out. When you meet a friend, you do not say, "Hello, Mary Delano Silvio," even though that is her full name. You say, "Hello, Mary." Mary knows exactly what you mean. How odd it would be for Mary if you used her whole name. It is the same with Spirit. When you say, "Spirit, I want a beautiful home with a large foyer for greeting guests, a kitchen decked out with Dakota granite …"

We say, "Don't you know us?" We bring you what you desire.

We know all that you desire—however, not just the details on the carpet color. We know the whole picture at all times. Where do you think that desire comes from in the first place? Yes, it is in Spirit, inspiration. We bore it in you on a level of your unawareness. So spell it all out if you must to make it clear to yourself. We know what you desire. Just allow it. Allow all you want to come to you by loving yourself and doing all you can to feel good.

Day 3

The mind does not work alone. It needs Spirit always. So the Spirit that is One is in all minds.

Spirit works in the mind to experience the physical world. We express Our desires in the physical through you. That's from Our perspective. From your perspective, if you know Us, you say you are inspired. If you are unaware of Us, you say you are ambitious. But understand this, for every desire that We have, We also have the tools to manifest it. It is because We are One—desire and fulfillment, the Alpha and the Omega. You are the vessel of that love and joy that We are here for.

Sometimes your mind convinces you that something cannot be done like that or you're not good enough to receive this. That is when you do not allow Us to come in and help you. That is when Our flow is stopped. We don't stop; We keep bringing forth ways to fulfill your/Our desire. But in most cases, a change in attitude must occur for you to see that, yes, you can, it can, it will be, and it now is.

We do not control you to force you to have what you want and do all you want. We offer the tools, and with your free will, you can use them or not use them. We always encourage you to use them.

Day 4

Your life is a gift. You receive it fully when you open your heart. Your life is forever unfolding.

Life is given to you. It is a present. Open the surprise today. How precious is your life? It is a gift in every sense of the word. It is given to you with all the splendor the universe has to offer.

You are born. Do you think you learn everything from a parent or guardian? Do you think you are a victim of environment or nurture? No, you are not a victim of all that. You are the opposite of all that. We can call you a m-i-t-c-i-v, reversing the letters of victim; for lack of a better word that is opposite to victim, we turn that word around for you. You are a creator.

With the spark of God inside, you come forth to experience the glorious wonder of creation through time. While you have choices, all is known where We are. You truly are along for the ride of a lifetime.

We give you life; without Us, dear one, you would be a bag of bones. We put the "oomph" in your body to get up in the morning, and the skip in your step when you are aligned with Us. You wonder, *Am I doing the right thing? Am I supposed to be doing this and not that?* Now, We ask you, "Do you feel good? Are you exhilarated?" That is your answer.

Day 5

You cannot *not* be connected to Spirit; We are here at all times.

All times. Even when you feel crappy, when you think people aren't treating you right, when you think things should be better. If you don't feel Us, then it is you who has lowered your vibration. And this is a good thing. Because—know this—in just seconds, not minutes, you can and will be connected to Us again.

Your mind asks, *Did I say the wrong thing? Did I do the wrong action?* No need to worry here. Remember, you are guided to do all. Some of it might not be the most appropriate way to do things, but in that wrong action, you learn a better action. Keep acting. Don't stop. It is constant learning and loving—constant learning to love yourself. We are not guiding you to do everything perfectly. We are guiding you so you have opportunities to learn.

Now, that part of you that thinks, *He doesn't like me*, and *I'm not good enough*, is ego making illusory comparisons. Flip the switch. Turn the light on. We are on a different wavelength and light level. Send light on that subject that is bothering you. Shed the light of Us on it. Flood it with light. The dark thought will disappear. Yes, We are light; We are love. And you are that too. We are that part of you connected to God/Source/All-That-Is, Was, and Will Be.

Spirit is with you at all times. We don't leave. You are never abandoned. Spirit is here, is here, and is here. Spirit is everywhere. And you are here experiencing all of it. But it is not a flower-petaled path; it is a path of learning. We encourage you to ride the wave—and also have fun doing it.

Day 6

My wisdom is of the ages. My wisdom is born of all experience that all beings have. Would it not benefit you to consult Us?

Life was meant for much joy. It saddens Us that many of you don't see that ever or many of you have forgotten that. Sometimes, you are blinded because of only one thing you are focused on: a hurt, a disappointment, or a loss. Beloveds, look to the joyful experience not the bummer experience. That's where I am.

I am not in the pain, although that pain makes room for Me eventually, because during your suffering, you lose focus on all of the other things—the minor things—that upset you. I will take any opening I can to get in and reach you. That is why so many people say, "God is in suffering." Yes, I am there in suffering because I am there always. But you see Me clearer because you lose sight of all the other trivial stuff you have been focused on.

Sometimes suffering is brought to you by your soul so, through it, you can learn that which is needed. Remember, your soul does not offer a rose-petaled path.

We would advise you to be open to Source at all times. And that means paying attention to the details. Notice the name of the cabdriver when you are sitting in the front seat; pick up on the unusual silence of your child. Be vigilant about being aware. Know why you are doing it and how it benefits us both.

I grow from your experiences. I am infinite wisdom, I am here to guide you, and I also learn. You and all beings offer the experiences that All-That-Is grows from. You are part of that matrix. What you learn is then offered up to Me to be returned to thee and thou.

How do you think I got so smart? Experience teaches. And I am the ultimate "experience witnesser."

Geri's Note: This information didn't seem to jive with what I had been taught. I was taught that God was out in the universe making judgments on what is right and what is wrong. If we behave and do what God wants us to do, we will get our just rewards and get to spend eternity with Him in heaven. But my beliefs do not coincide with what is coming through now. Source is now saying that we are part of the development of Him. I ask some questions for clarification and maybe understanding.

Geri: Are you not more than that, my Lord?

Spirit: More than what, Gerardette [my given name]? Am I not more than you, yourself? I am Lord, having experiences through all beings. I am both the Initiator of the experience and the "Experiencer" of that gift. You are the physicality from which I express. You and all beings are representations of *Me*.

Geri: Then, to my background and thought, that seems like you are controlling me.

Spirit: I have the controls; there is no doubt about that. But unlike a video game, you have free will. That is why you see so many addicted to alcohol or other things as they decide not to listen to the inner voice.

You look at My explanation as a wrong in that you think I am pulling puppet strings. I offer you and all beings the gift of life. Follow Me, and I will bring you a wonderful life. I would have it no other way. I cannot desire suffering for you. It is not in Me. That comes from your own beliefs of life/experience without connection to Me.

You are a major in the equation. And if you know that, accept me as the General. I am the Generator of All-That-Is and I am the Recipient of All-That-Is. Ah, can you not feel my magnificence? Can you not see why I am pure love? I have it all. And you do too when you align with My idea for you. There's nothing to figure out. Be open. Love, and I will guide you there—not like a puppet but like a partner. We join to experience your life. Keep Me close, and it will be a meaningful journey.

Fear not for those who don't keep Me close. This life is a blink of the eye of experience. We will be joined soon enough with that one who doesn't keep Me close. You see, he will be magnificent soon. Don't deny your abundance while here because of someone else. You came here to experience all that We desire for you. Believe Us; that is not chump change. It is love, beauty, joy, and good feeling thoughts that We want for you and all human beings.

Geri: Some get tired, bored with Your message, especially in places like church.

Spirit: No need to get tired of Me. I am infinite. I say, "OK, I'll sit back and you pick. You decide what to do with your life." Always, you pick something smaller than what I want to give you. Please understand infinite wisdom. It is all-knowing, and in that are all the riches of all the kingdoms. Believe Me; I do not refer to all the gold the greedy ones hide in their underground vaults, more gold than they can use in ten thousand lifetimes. That is misguided. Infinite wisdom brings out that which you need to live on and that which you need to grow. It is a wealth of experience of love to draw from. In that (infinite wisdom), We create the universe and your universe. With this particular life and with the backing of All-That-Is, the universe truly can move mountains.

Watch, and you will see. And do not ever become impatient. All things come to he who waits. And all things are on My time for the best good for all.

Day 7

Vibrate on the level of love, and all will be open to you.

I am always here. You tried to write earlier but could not because your vibration was not in the place where you can translate My words. Where you were, you couldn't hear them. I was with you, but you were not with Me fully.

Geri's Note: I was in a funk and could not get messages from Spirit. I wanted to know what was going on, what was different about my experience, so I asked the question and a flood of information came to me.

Geri: What happened? How come it wasn't flowing like the first four days?

Spirit: You were nervous because you told people about the project. You even called a literary agent. *Oo-oo-oo-oo scary stuff,* you may have thought for some moments. Know that I am with you when you are scared. But know too you do not have access to My thoughts when you are nervous or afraid, because I am the opposite of that. I am love. Turn those letters around, and you have evol—evolve, evolution.

You are in the midst of a glorious evolution, dear one and all readers. You have access; all of you have more access to other dimensions of living. It is heart-centered. The energy of the heart is flooding your planet, and it will change the way you live. Thankfully, most of you are saying, because it would not be, if it were not first desired.

Many of you, for a long, long time, have hoped to have a more caring society. In the greedy world that you were part of, where was the help for the children? Now, children who needed more help had to come to your world to help you change your focus.

Believe Me; all happens for a reason. Are not those children who need extra help the most loving at times? And happy! They vibrate so much more happiness than many so-called healthy children and adults.

Children are here to teach us many things. Happiness, we would say, is among the top five. Others we would include are service and togetherness in family, patience, and love, to name a few.

Let's talk about service and its connection to Source. You cannot feel closer to Source without service. Think about it; is service not what All-That-Is is all about? I serve you. Everything you want, I line up for you. You don't get it all right away, and some of it you never get. You never get it because you never "get it." That is, you never give up your fear and negative thoughts. We say you never get it. But that's not true. Be very sure that you will get it and all that is lined up for you as soon as you leave the physicality and the limiting thoughts therein. You see, there is much power in "allowing" right now all good things to come as requested.

Think about what I do. I made you in My likeness. Now, think about what you do. Do you serve other human beings? Do you offer them help, a hand, or even a smile? Think of how lovely it would be if you were not on guard all the time. So many people are protecting their hearts, preventing them from opening up to their coworkers, neighbors, and even family members.

We feel that all is certainly getting better, but there are a few holdouts. They will change, or they will not be in the same dimension as most on the planet. What does that mean? It does not mean that they will be plucked from their environment and put into a burning hell. Psychologically or emotionally, they will keep themselves in the dimension they resonate with. That means they will be in *their* physical world, but the law of attraction will bring them by you less and less. Think of Dante's *Inferno* and his nine layers of hell. Think of these layers as energy dimensions in which one is trapped because of one's actions or behavior (always born of thought) of greed, jealousy, and all the other behaviors that cut us off from love. Locked in one of *these* attitudes, we will resonate on that level, the same world—same physical world—different energetic dimension.

Geri's Note: Now we return to the message I believe Spirit intended.

My message for you today is: "Be aware of what dimension you are thinking/feeling/expressing on." Your anxiety about the project caused you to be unable to have access to My thought-download to you.

Do you see how wonderfully orchestrated that is, to teach us a lesson? Not in the sense of a negative lesson, but to make it clear to you. This has been a glorious unfolding too. It started yesterday when you were moved to talk about this project. Who moved you? Who inspired you? We did. We did this to show you how anxiety and fear creep up when you lock yourself into a project. No matter. The project will get done one day or another day, after you take the anxiety and fear away from it.

My message is: Vibrate on the level of love (not fear) and all will be open to you. You will have access, loving access, to Me and My power of Source. That means all things will come to you. This is what I do. I serve you. When you serve others, you are acting in My likeness.

Geri's Note: My fear continued, and my methodical brain wondered why I was getting more than one message in one day when the project was named "Forty Days and Forty Nights with Spirit." I assumed I would get forty messages in forty days. But that was not the case. In the end, the forty messages took less than two weeks. The next day, Spirit tried to put me back on track.

Day 8

The joy is in the journey.

Loved one, you are in danger of losing the essence of this project. You were not to set all on forty days and forty nights, counting the words and days and determining when you will be done. You'll be done when you're done—when *We* are done. Do not push it along. And do not stop while waiting for the next day. There is much to say to you and all human beings. And this morning, I remind you: the joy is in the journey. Love the now, and don't worry about what is to come. It will be there when you need it.

We are not abandoning you. Keep your vibration with Ours. There is enough information to fill thousands—an infinite number, really—of books. Our experiences, past, present, and future, are varied and experienced differently by the multitudes. There are some who see Us in words, others who hear Us in music, and still others who feel Us as We dance around them.

There will never be a time when We stop giving you information. When you don't hear Us, the question to ask yourself is: *Am I allowing it?* Are you letting it in, dear one?

You are not on this project to count the letters and weigh the paragraphs. You are here for the information. Listen to Us, and find the joy in the journey.

Day 9

If a thought does not serve you well, discard it. You *are* your thoughts.

Some of you worry about others controlling you. You don't want anybody (any "body" or any "thing") controlling your thoughts and actions. We see you controlled by your own thoughts. Your negative thoughts enslave you to a negative world. You are chained to it. You won't look at or imagine a better world out of habit, clinging instead to a negative thought or belief.

We say: Clear your mind of the negativity first, and then you will see how free you really can be. Let go of the thought that makes you feel bad about yourself, your house, your loved ones. See them all in a different light.

Sometimes, you cling to "Oh, woe, he did this ..." and "She did that to me." All of that is negative energy, your negative energy. If it's affecting you and making you present a negative energy or vibration, We see *you* as the one with the "problem." The other person is going on about his day, even though you say he wronged you; We don't see that. We see your ire, and only ire can We return onto you. So no matter the circumstance—if it's *your* feeling and *your* reaction, *you* own it. And since you own it, you control that. You control the negative thoughts. Turn that thought around and then the next one. Make one change of focus at a time, and you will contribute to a better life experience.

Geri's Note: I am reminded of a vision I received when my neighbors' dogs bothered me so much. I was so angry that my neighbors did not pick up the dogs' business. A vision came to me that what was being seen in a higher dimension was not my neighbors' sloppiness, but my own nasty reaction to it. In my vision, I saw myself throwing poop toward my neighbors' yard. I had to protest that energetic interpretation. I explained to Spirit that it was my neighbors who were being unkind. But what the Spirit world experienced was me being unkind, dishing out the negative feelings I had about my neighbors. Today, it would serve me better if I tried to soften my approach and imagined a time when I would tell my neighbors when it was time for them to clean their yard if I was irked by the smell. However I deal with it, one thing is certain: I don't want to be seen as a negative influence in this world or the energetic world.

Day 10

Do unto others as you would have them do unto you.

"I am music, and I write the songs." You get that, don't you? You know what that means. We are music; We write the songs. You download them. We are beauty. We desire beauty in this world. And so be it.

To the greatest sculptors, We gave this plan: chip away what is not needed for this vision We give thou. Some of the greatest masters knew where this art and beauty came from. They publicly attributed their work *in Deo*, to God. They knew it was all God.

Glory to God in the Highest. Have you not heard the choir of angels sing this?

Geri's Note: Source is referencing an experience I had, which you may have had as well. This one—the choir of angels singing. I heard it one morning, and it reverberated through my head and my being. It was a joyful, otherworldly experience.

All can hear it, if they are vibrating at that level. That song, written by the angels, translated centuries ago, continues to be sung today because We inspire it to be sung. It is sung in your church. Your church triggered the angels' music in your head. Was it in your head? Or was it all around you? You woke up one morning, and the choirs of angels were singing all around you. You can't say it was inside your head, can you? You still feel it surrounding your head. The most beautiful heavenly sound: "Glory to God in the highest." Was it a thousand angels singing?

You know God exists. When you create, what will you do? Will you credit Him/Her? Will you attribute all your grand work to God? That's what the angels sing about. They attribute everything, *everything* to Me. Now, what of the so-called bad work? Do you attribute that to God as well? That we may save for another day.

Geri's Note: Spirit and I enter into an even more specific conversation, which follows if you are interested. If not, jump to day 11.

Spirit: Will you remember that all is God? Once you were incensed about a writer who survived death under the most unlikely circumstances, you saw God's hand in it completely. But that author did not write about God's hand in his life. That incensed you. Will you do the same? So many do. It takes much courage and faith to say that it is all God's work, and in that you, too, friend, sister, brother can do the same as I. How will you ascribe the miracles? Will you call it your Higher Self? Your Source? Your God?

Geri: How would you like me to say it?

Spirit: We think it necessary to thank Spirit. This is an introduction to the world, to the Word. Tell the world that Spirit speaks these words. Spirit wrote this.

Geri: And why?

Spirit: Because We want all to recognize We are here. We can help you understand your life and help you define "human being."

Geri: What is a human being?

Spirit: One who loves himself, loves others, and loves life; one who finds beauty in music and in the rain; one who rejoices doing certain music melodies; and one who flies through the dimensions with the greatest of ease; one who dances with Spirit; one who follows Spirit's lead; one who delights in all that is here because all that is here is good.

Geri: What do you want?

Spirit: We want you to be happy. Yes, for your sake. But We are part of you and We feel you. We want you ruled more by joy than by money, more by love than by fear, and more by what feels right and good than by what doesn't. We want you to be whole and healthy, and We will tell you how to do that.

Geri: How, Lord?

Spirit: By believing that you can be or do or have anything you want and by believing the same for all others; by allowing what you desire to come to you, and by doing all in your power to become happy.

Geri: Are you going to give us examples?

Spirit: Yes. I will give examples.

Listen to each other. How often do you enter into conversation where both talk at the same time? Have you heard what the other said? Have an interest in the other, a curiosity of the other. Open your heart to the other.

"Why?" you may ask. Not for the other's benefit, although it is evident how the other benefits. Do it for yourself. Open yourself to the other, and it comes back to you. Spirit bounces. If you give love to others, it returns to you. That is the nature of God, love. In sharing love, you receive love. And that's the greatest gift of being human.

When you share love, you share Me. When you give Me, you receive Me. It's an elasticity of energy that resounds or rebounds and reverberates between humans. We bounce back and forth through the heart center. And that, dearest loved one, is the dance!

The Dance (as described in Sydney Lok's *The Dance of the Golden Bow*) is the physical movement of the bouncing of love—of the infinity of our joined love. The orb, the figure eight, circulates through us as you trace the circles, you see.

Geri's Note: "The Dance" is a moving meditation designed to connect you to Higher Self. You can find more information on Sydney and "The Dance" on Joy Media's website www.joymediaonline.com. This was Joy Media's first project and is offered as a DVD.

That is why you resonated so with *The Dance*. It is Our dance. We join you when you do it. We join you anyway. But doing *the dance* joins us physically and emotionally. It binds us together. It is ritual, and there is joy in that ritual. It acknowledges that you love Us and We love you.

The orb, the infinity symbol, the figure eight, is infinite love, you see. We like to demonstrate it. And you call Us forth every time you do *the dance*. It is natural to be with you this way. It is an ecstasy for Us, and when you are pure of heart, it is an ecstasy for you as well.

Now you worry you will sound like the "Popeil Pocket Fisherman" because you offer "The Dance" here in this book and on your website. Young one, where did you get such ideas that selling is bad? This brings us to our message today. Take a belief, any belief. In your case, "selling is sleazy." (Reader, please visit your own belief that needs changing. You will know what it is because I will tell you. Sit quietly for five minutes, and I will tell you what that belief is that needs changing. Remember, your beliefs can keep you small. You may be shocked to your core about the belief that is limiting you.)

Now, Geri, "The Dance" is a modern movement that will help human beings/people get close to Us and thereby closer to themselves. We are part of you; you cannot separate from Us. You can ignore Us, and you see how that is working for you—we think, not very well.

"The Dance," the infinity of Our love for you is the golden rule, you see. "Do unto others as you would have them do unto you." It is expressed in the physical movement. Is it becoming clear now? Do you know what our message is today?

Geri: Yes, Lord.

Spirit: And, reader, are you ready? (We pause for the reader to recite along.)

The Golden Rule: Do unto others as you would have them do unto you. Love your neighbor as yourself. As it is in the physical, so it is in the spiritual and vice versa. Others say it this way: What goes around comes around. Blessings to you, Geri, and to you, reader.

So in this lesson, We talk of erroneous core beliefs and eliminating them with love.

Take your core belief about selling. Why do you think it is sleazy? Was it the Fuller Brush man supposedly preying on the women in the neighborhood? Was it the Avon lady or the Tupperware parties? We bless salesmen. We think some of those products make life easier. You have a right to your opinion. But when you offer a product to someone who needs it, there's no greater service. We do it all the time.

We offer you things you need all the time. Do we ask for something in return? You bet We do, and it's more than the exchange of money. We ask for your attention and your growth and your joy. In the physical, there is an exchange as well. Sometimes, it's money, and sometimes, it's an exchange of service. Either way, it is always an exchange of energy. It is quite natural, you see. This gives, and that takes. Sometimes, you are on the giving stage and sometimes on the taking stage. In sales, you are on the giving stage. You are offering a product in service to another, an opportunity for the other. Please look at it that way. You are not taking from their lives. You are offering. It's up to them to accept or not accept. As long as you offer with love, you will be an effective salesperson. Sell to others, and they sell to you. The physical exchange of money is so minor. The exchange of ideas and services is the focus, dear one. The money is minor. Major is the exchange with love.

Day 11

Worry not what others think; it is you who creates your world.

Sometimes you worry what another might say about your choices. I say I gave *you* life. Choose as you and I would decide. Others have no idea about our idea or our plan. Let them talk.

"What? You are not going for that job?"

"What? You are marrying that man?"

"Don't you know there's more money in the other job?"

"Don't you know he's a different race?"

And then they say if it's not you who will be unhappy, surely your children will be most miserable.

Beloveds, do not listen to them. The naysayers will rob you of your life. Instead, trust your feelings. If something just feels right to you, it is right. It is so simple. Good feels good and bad, well, not so much.

You and I are planning and participating in this life—not your mother, neighbor, or coworker. You know I am not saying to be disrespectful of their thoughts and opinions. You know I am saying to respect your own choices and what we create together.

Day 12

Clean up your house; address the negative aspects of yourself that keep you small.

Friends, We are here to make life better for you. We ask you to stretch your imagination. What if there was no world? How would you create it?

This We tell you now: you cannot hide your thoughts or feelings under a bushel anymore. Was there ever a time you could hide them? Not really from Us, but from each other, yes. You were hiding from each other.

We say now, let your light so shine. The reason We say this is because it *will* shine. All pretenses will drop away in the physical world. You see that already in your religions, economy, and now yourselves, children. You will wake totally nude—void of any coverings of your feelings. We advise you to act now.

Address the negative aspects of yourself that keep you small. Now is the time. There will soon come a time when all of that which you are will be known to all. It is already known to All-That-Is. We say it will be known to all of you. The secret veils you have put up to hide from each other will be lifted.

Hence, our message: clean up your house. Do due diligence. Make right your wrongs, if not with others, then at least within yourself. It is time now to do so.

We warn, the energy that comes soon will purge the negative for sure, but it will be painful, so painful, without your awareness and acknowledgment. Please don't fight the cosmos. The Universe is moving at its time, and it's time to pay the piper. It's not a bad thing. Don't you think the piper should be paid for His music?

Acknowledge that the life you have is given to you by the Creator. You create by aligning with All-That-Is. It's a joint venture that cleans your soul as the universe works its magic through you.

All is good. This is a natural process. It will ready you for what is to come.

Geri's Note: I take the opportunity to ask Spirit a bit about the future.

Geri: Well, what is to come?

Spirit: A new world. It is a new world order, one that is not enmeshed in secrets, pain, and deceit.

Geri: Must we all go through this process?

Spirit: Most, not all. There are some among you who are already close to God in that they care about humans and are not greedy and love each other. All others must start addressing the issues within their own persons.

Geri: How does one start?

Spirit: Make a list. On that list should be all life experiences that you felt hurt you. Examine, one by one, each of these circumstances. How did each one unfold? How do you see it? How would the other person involved see it? How did you contribute to making it a hurtful situation?

When you realize that the situation or event that you have been hanging onto for decades was actually something you yourself requested, you will be able to let go and let God. You will feel the joy of experiencing the lifting of that negative energy you held onto for dear life. We call this the "cleansing process." Do it now for all experiences. It will take most people at least a month. After that, do it daily—release things as they come up. This will serve you well in the times to come.

Geri's Note: there is a cleansing process worksheet at the end of this section of the book to help with this process.

Day 13

There is always conflict. Resolving the conflict with ease brings you close to who *We* are and what *you* want.

We are the diffusers of conflict, you could say. We don't weigh the result bit by tiny bit. We look at the vibrational content of what goes this way and then send more of it that direction.

We sway with the law of attraction. We see an opening somewhere, and We swoop in. We register your thoughts, words, and actions and give it a vibrational frequency. That ensures that you get more of the same.

Conflict is inevitable. Learn to sway with conflict, to live with conflict, to be comfortable in the midst of conflict. Conflict is your home. Keep your vibration attuned to where *We* are, and you will avoid the drama of the conflict. Let it be. Let all get what each one wants and work together. That is how it is in Spirit. Each bit of energy has its space, and each other bit of energy sways this way or that way or joins with another piece of energy to create layers and deeper, more powerful energies. You cannot join with unlike energy here. It is a complete openness. There, you can be fooled and join with unlike energy because an energy fooled you or, after the fact, changed its focus. Here, there is pure energy, pure knowledge of who or what that being wants and the question, "Is this a good fit?" Energies know. Many humans don't know, but if they listen to their inner selves, they will choose to join with energy like themselves.

Today's message is: let it be. Conflict in the world is inevitable and necessary. It is desire born of conflict that is one of the largest creators on Earth. Let it be. Move over. Let the conflict resolve into a magnificent result. But don't get stuck in the drama. There, in the drama, you can languish without ever reaching the benefit of that which was born. Being in the drama stops the result from coming to you—like a glass wall stops the bird from entering your porch. You can see it, but it cannot come to you. Your vibration in the drama is not lined up with the dream.

Dream big, and limit the drama, We would advise. And in conflict, let the chips fall where they may. Do not have attachment to where they fall.

Day 14

Enjoy the moment. It is here you find the essence of your life.

Pay attention to the mint smell of the shampoo, the way your legs feel relaxing on your bed. Breathe in the magnificence of the fresh air in the woods. Pay attention to the detail of the moment. Can you hear the music? Is it silent? Is there a rhythm to the cars traveling on the highway in the distance? Do you see the full loving body of your sons, a friend, a loving grandma in your home? Can you sit and feel All-That-Is inside that being, that sound, that room? All-That-Is is here right now.

All-That-Is is all around you. You can feel the Creator in the stillness of the moment. You can feel this "now" moment for eternity. Each moment is a gift of forever.

Day 15

There is no bad, and there is no good. In heaven, all exists harmoniously.

Now the challenge, My friends, is this: if you think and label yourself good or better than another or even the best, then you must label someone bad, worse, or the worst. Labeling yourself and defining yourself in this way does not serve you well.

We have told you that you create with Us. Our desires take hold of you. Some called the famous president George Bush the Darth Vader of your world. Now, others use that term for Barack Obama. Others label their boss as such. Hear Me now: No one is better or worse than you. All people act as inspired to act based on the law of like energies. We won't go into the politics of either red or blue, but We will tell you We like the color purple.

Can you not, if you are the color red, look at blue and say, "I like that part of blue," and vice versa if you are blue? Can't we all be different shades of purple? Limit taxes and take care of those who can't take care of themselves? We say yes, you can. In fact, you can do it without paying any taxes at all.

The people you elect must be people of new vision. Those people see the waste and greed, and they must stop it. You must absolutely demand this of your leaders.

Our message this morning: there is no bad, and there is no good. In heaven, all exists harmoniously. We all understand each other's perspective, and We move with the energy of that perspective. Energies preferring that way flow that way; energies preferring what we ourselves like flow toward Us.

There is no judgment where We are. No bad and no good either. Stop dividing yourselves as such. Most of you have gotten over the black-and-white thing and replaced it with blue and red. Stop it. Let's say we are all purple and various shades of it; some violet, others periwinkle. But we are all the color purple. We are all one. Us here, and you there, you there and you there—all one, each one whole and holy. Treat each other accordingly.

Day 16

When raising children, take a step back. Don't do everything for them. They have their own guidance.

Yes, it is a good thing that you are not pouring his juice in the morning.

Geri's Note: Spirit is referring to my high-school senior son who leaves for school at 6:50 a.m.

You felt it wasn't right to cater to him, that he would be upset. It didn't feel right for him, either. He knew it wasn't good that you poured his juice in the morning; that's why he was nasty. His guidance was telling him, "Mom shouldn't be doing this for me. If I want juice, I'll pour it myself."

When raising children, step back. Of course, know when to step in, in case of potential harm. But in general, take a step back when raising children. Let them do for themselves and make their own decisions. It is better in the long run.

In the short run and especially when they are short ones, it is easier to clean up their messes and decide things for them. But don't do that. Take a step back, even when they are younger, and let them do for themselves.

Day 17

If I am Infinite Wisdom, you offer loving faith. We fit together nicely.

I offer you all these words and more. I offer you music and painting and accounting. I offer you the natural beauty of trees and forests and streams. I offer you seasons of expressions of love in the summer and especially in the fall. How much do you love the snow I give you when it sits on top of the pine tree in the quiet of the afternoon? Yes, I even give you words of poetry.

What do you give Me? You give me yourself. You give me the faith that I will do your will, dear one. I am here to offer you what your bigger self wants to experience. Any question you have, I have an answer. Any experience you want, I can give you. In order to do this, loved one, you must have faith that I can deliver. Do have faith, loved one, because indeed faith can move mountains.

Have you not heard the story of a young girl living in poverty in Chicago? Her family was so desperate, and she reached out to whom? To Me. She reached out to Me and believed I could make her life better. And so it was done. It had to be. In no time, Jennifer Hudson received fame and an Oscar. It can be done. It has been done. How will you partner your faith with My abilities?

Believe. Imagine. Cocreate with Me. It is joyous for you, and it is joyous for Me. This is how We meant you to live when you were created—experiencing the joys of the physical world through Spirit's eyes. Now you tell Me, what can be better than that, here on earth or even here in heaven?

Day 18

Always and everywhere give thanks.

You don't often think of it; many never think of it: the miracle of you. Always give thanks. Thank God for the day, the night, and everything in between. The sun, the star shine, the experiences of this life—it is all a miracle. And these experiences are finite. Thank God for the difficulties as well. They serve to teach you wondrous things.

Here's the thing: I always and everywhere give thanks for you, and look where I am. Appreciation serves you most well. So go about your day giving thanks. Thank you, Geri, for penning my words.

Geri's Note: At this moment, Spirit and I enter into a specific conversation about what this project is and I wonder if there will be more projects. It follows here if you are interested.

Geri: Thank you, Lord, for inspiring me to do this project.

Spirit: There is a lot here but still so much more to say.

Geri: Even though we are only on day 18, I am looking ahead. Will there be another forty days and forty nights?

Spirit: Maybe. No one can predict the future. Remember, there are only possibilities. We would say yes, it is possible. That is how cocreation works. You never fully know how I will participate, only that I will be there. The same for you. Will it be what you desire?

Geri: Did I desire this?

Spirit: In the worst way. How many times did you pick up a Bible and say, "Why is this not easier to read?" *This* book, Geri's Bible, is born of the desire you have for understanding *that* book. You really could call this Geri's Bible if you wanted. But I'll leave that part to you.

Geri: Geri's Bible. That will take a while to sink in.

Spirit: What do you think those stories [the Bible stories] were for? For teaching. In those days, lessons were taught with stories. Then Jesus perfected the parable. You are presenting more instructions, a sort of handbook for this day.

Geri: Why me? Can anyone else write their own Bible?

Spirit: You, because of the longing and desire and the allowing. Yes, readers anywhere can write their own Bible. It is encouraged.

Day 19

With regard to the children, stop worrying about them and spend more time enjoying them.

The children are your blessings. Treat them as such. They put the joy in the world with their tiny feet, little hands, and the things they say. They are the most precious of beings.

Don't harden them too early. In fact, don't harden them at all. Laugh with them and not at them; talk to them and not for them. Watch them closely, for they are giving you so much more than you give them.

You give them a warm place to sleep and a good meal to eat. But man does not live on bread alone. Your children invite Spirit with every step because of their innocence. And the angels love to play with them. Sit near a child, and you sit closer to Me. I am so much more accessible in the lightheartedness of the young ones. We can feel a laugh coming from miles away, and We want to be there when it explodes. It is a true feeling here—a little explosion when children laugh. Enjoy them; they are heaven-sent.

Day 20

Free will is Our gift to you, and it trumps all others anywhere in the universe.

Children, a very powerful creative tool was given to you because of My deep love and appreciation for you.

Dear ones, I made you in My likeness and cannot *not* give you the power to decide for yourselves. Oh, what a headache I gave myself, you could say.

But I don't see it that way, really. I gave you free will so you could decide whether to join Me or not. If you have a better idea, go for it. If you are not ready for Me, I will wait.

Free will, like freedom, is a double-edged sword. In free will, you get to do as you please. But don't you know the only way to please yourself is to join with Spirit, who can help you become magnificent?

Free will allows you to say, "No!" But loved one, keep saying no and that is all that is returned to you. Say, "Yes! Yes, I will do that job. Yes, I will play that game. Yes, I will offer you my time."

Then, when you get there, decide if you will continue. Do not say, "No, no, no." Then what We must return to you is the same.

Allow your free will to be free of won't. You have free will to say, "Yes, I will." Believe us; it is in your will that all comes.

Some keep all the stuff from coming to them by saying, "No." By saying, "No," you disallow. And you no longer have free will. What you have is slavery to negativity.

Your free will was created so that you could grow to think and do like Me. I say, "Yes," to everything. To all things, I say, "Yes." I make no judgments. Will you say, "Yes," to only one thing? I ask you to say, "Yes," to Me and I will show you what free will can do. I have the power to make all dreams come true. Say, "Yes," to that. Right now, reader, say, "Yes," to Me.

Chapter Two

Love

TAKING A BREATHER

After twenty messages, I'm taking a breather. Join me for some reflection on where we are, where we came from, and where we are going. And let's also celebrate the first twenty messages.

"Oh, we're halfway there. Aha, we're living on a prayer." Bon Jovi sang this the other night on the Grammy Awards. I sang the refrain throughout the night and into the next day. At times, I picked up a glass, pretending it was a microphone. While I sang it around the house, my son told me he had just downloaded that song onto his iPod. That is an example of synchronicity. Once I started listening to Spirit, I began experiencing synchronicity all the time like this. And now that I am halfway through this book, of course, I hear that song several times. It's no surprise to me anymore. I smile and say, "Thank you. I get it. We are halfway there!"

Halfway through this cocreation with Spirit, first called, "Forty days and Forty nights: What All-That-Is Wants All of Us to Know." How am I feeling? And what is going on with me now that twenty days and twenty nights have been written?

First, how am I feeling? I am feeling as if my insides are being turned outside. I feel like my heart is being pried open and exposed. I feel that a lot of the clogging is being unclogged. I feel that I am opening my heart and accepting more about myself and about others—mostly about myself. Because I now understand that if I can understand myself, I can have better relationships with others.

During this process, several memories came up, as did several realizations and reactions to my everyday life. I'll take memories first. I'll give you one example. When the message about how Spirit sees you came up, I was reminded about the vision I had last summer. I wrote about it earlier and will explain more now.

At that time, I complained to anyone who would listen about the awful smell in my backyard caused by the neighbors' dogs. Our houses are next to each other, and their poop garden is right by my fence. The vision I had one night was a picture of me on my backyard porch throwing piles of poop at my neighbors' yard. When I woke up, I said, "Wait a minute, Spirit. You have it wrong here. It is them, my neighbors, who are shoveling the poop my way." Later, I realized that Spirit saw my reaction to my neighbor and how They saw me was tossing the crap to my neighbor. "Not fair!" I shouted for weeks. "That's not how it is. That's not the reality of it." Finally, I decided to make peace with it. For me, it was looking away and holding my breath every time I passed that part of the yard. I didn't have the nerve to confront my neighbor, but I did soften my reaction to the dogs. By the way, eventually, my neighbor put up a fence that made things much better for me.

The realizations I have had include how wonderful my life is right now. I now realize that I don't need all my dreams to come true to have a wonderful, magical life. It is here right now. I think about my children mostly, how beautiful they are inside and out. I think about how I love to speak with them, share my thoughts, and listen to theirs. Even when they are not being terribly patient with me, they are relating to me in a way that is unique in the universe. I am so blessed to have such loving beings around me. It blows my mind how much my husband loves me and how much his parents, my parents, my sisters and brothers, and the people I say "hello" to at work love me. They love me in a unique way only humans can love, and it's evidenced in a smile, a handshake, and a shared joke. It is so magnificent.

Another thing I am realizing is how reactionary I can become when things don't go my way. In the past few days, I have had a particularly challenging experience with a vendor who wants one thing while I want another. The information from Spirit about conflict has helped me in this one. Big-time. I am honoring myself mostly. This is what's so unusual. Usually, I would just give in without considering my needs. Now, I am examining my needs and mostly trying to let the situation ride out and resolve itself. I don't know how it will turn out, but I am turning inward and letting the chips fall where they may. It's a matter of being comfortable with uncertainty. If I am in disagreement with you, it doesn't have to be resolved immediately. I can honor where I stand and not cave in to others' demands.

This half of the book has been fascinating to me. But I also find it embarrassing. The stuff about selling *The Dance* makes me feel uncomfortable. My intention with the book was to share what Spirit says, but I have found much of it to be of a personal nature. I am going with it and sharing my personal stuff because I think that's how we learn: by looking at others' experiences and comparing them to our own. I'm grateful to other writers who share their experiences and help me understand my own life.

In spite of some fear and trepidation, I continue to be excited about this project. I asked Spirit, "Where are we going?" What came through is more of the nitty-gritty. Spirit is going to show us how to live better by changing our thoughts about one thing at a time. So let's move to the second half of the messages from Spirit.

Chapter Three

THE NEXT TWENTY
MESSAGES

Day 21

In the beginning, there was the Word and It was good.

Do you know, loved ones, that here good means God? In the beginning, there was the Word. And All-That-Is was the Word. When spoken, it became "world." That's how the world was created. It was created when I spoke the Word. The Word became the world. It was an explosion of thought into action, Spirit into physical. I thought it up. Really, I did.

In the beginning, there was just God. And the truth is all is still the same today. There is just God. All is God. Nothing is separated from Me. Everything is Me, and I am all else.

So you could say God is the good, the bad, and the ugly, and I would say, "Yes, I am. I am all that. That I am. *I am that I am.*"

Day 22

You would do well to be more like Me. Have fewer judgments, and be more of service.

I implore you to be more like Me. You are My children. Don't parents want their children to be the apple of their eye, a chip off the old block?

But honestly, children, it is mostly the other way around with you and Me. I want to learn from you. I grow from you. You grow Me. Inside you, I grow. It is the God molecule in you that grows through experience.

Day 23

Listen to yourself, beloveds. All that is in you will come out in your words.

Make this a Valentine's Day for yourself. I implore you to love yourself. Here's a baby step: listen to yourself. There is so much you can learn from what you say.

Listen, not only to your brothers and sisters but also to yourself. What are you saying? Think about your words. They were born of your thoughts. Do your words come from a place of love or a place of fear?

Now, here's the rub: say your discontent, give it voice and energy, and more will come to you. Have you listened to yourself? Do you think you speak words of encouragement? Listen again. Are you putting someone down with your words? If so, know you are putting yourself down. We say now and again and again: "You are all one. We are all One. We cannot be separated."

Your words will tell you who you are and what you are thinking. Instead of the closets, clean up that area of your life. Clean up the words you use to describe your life, your loved ones, and your own self.

Day 24

Live with integrity. You will find it as the one thing that will help you sleep at night.

Beloveds, you won't need the wine, the pills, and the obsessive sex to relax. You will be relaxed if you stay true to yourself. We are not saying don't participate in those things; We implore you not to *absolutely* need them to get by. What is the fun in that?

Tell people how you feel. Warn people about your suspicions. Be open. If you are wrong, it is still good. We say it is very good. You get your feelings out in the open, and that is to be celebrated because then they won't fester. When there is nothing festering in your body or on your mind, you will sleep well and even be healthier, you see.

Let your thoughts out—air them out. Let the air take the dampness out of the cloak of secrecy. Fear not being wrong. Speak your piece/peace.

Day 25

Where two or more are gathered, I am there.

You cannot escape Me, beloveds. I am there. The question is: are you aware? Are you aware that I exist to serve you?

Jesus said, "Where two or more are gathered in My name, there is love." Beloveds, you are one and I am two. We do not need a meeting of this number or that number. We are joined. We are gathered already. We can create miracles together. Do not doubt this, for it is true.

Jesus spoke My Word. Many forget that He represented Me. Many want to see Jesus, the Son, when they leave this world. I say God the Father will greet you. If you insist, Jesus will be the go-between for you. I tell you now: you can come directly to Me. No middleman is needed.

Jesus was a teacher for a different world than you now live in. I speak to you through many teachers to tell you this: "Graduate, loved ones. Bypass the human Jesus, and join with God the Father, God the Mother, and God the Son. All of Us."

There is one-stop shopping to My heart. I am here. My heart is open. And what about yours? Will you connect directly to My love or leave it to a parent, My priest, rabbi, or imam, to bring you closer to Me? Dear one, I give you permission to come to Me directly. I am here.

Day 26

We are all One; the Internet was created to show you electronically we are all connected. We are so in Spirit as well.

For instance, you don't like that man at work? He can read your e-mails. On a global level, you're cutting that country out of your plans—its members will hack into your computer and try to destroy your business.

The Internet brings you electronically closer together. An electrical connection exists; it marries your brain circuitry. The mind is a terrible thing to waste. Without realization of the connection, you think you are acting alone. Think for a moment. You have heard that when a butterfly flaps its wings in one place, a major change occurs in another place. Let me say right now, this is a metaphor for what can happen when one person changes his or her attitude. The change in the butterfly effect is real. Think about the effect a change in your mind will have on the planet. I tell you now the change on the planet is noticeable. Will you be the one to change your attitude to a more positive outlook today?

Change your thought or attitude where you are now, and people around the world will feel it. It has that large of an effect. Many of your thoughts are not conducive to working together. Think about society. What thoughts do you have about a foreign country? We say that country is already feeling it—and reacting to it. Why, you ask, would some want to destroy the Internet? Why would someone want to take down the Twin Towers? It is because they see those things as symbols of greed. They cannot compete in a world that is stacked against them.

They cannot get what they want in this world so they wish to create a new one. They want a world without the financial restrictions of the United States and its allies. They want a world without the dominance of one society over all others.

Now, I say, what about you? How is the competitive thing working for you? Are you having a better life scratching and clawing for only morsels? Believe Me; I see all. I see you who are competing so hard, thinking you are coming away with more than the other. Believe Me; it is only crumbs that are being tossed. The world is so much more than what you have been pigeonholed into believing.

The world needs to allow democracies to thrive. The world also needs to allow other governments to thrive. The people of the world don't need to change the governments; they need to change themselves and then the leaders. Every one of you could start by imagining being ruled by or electing leaders with benevolent leanings. That is the first step.

But where is the drama in that? Some live for drama within families and within societies in your world. Don't partake in the drama, anywhere, and you will live better—no drama within yourself or among your families or your coworkers. That's a big start. That leads to no drama within your society, your country, and eventually your world.

Trust Me when We say this: you can make a difference. Change your thoughts and you can change your world. I kid you not.

Day 27

It's time to talk about your relationship with your body. Your body is temporary. You will not have it forever. Treat it as a guest.

If a friend were visiting, you would make him or her feel comfortable. Think of your body as your friend. And think of your true self as the host. Be kind to your body. Offer it food and drink and conversation. Listen to your body. Stop forcing things in front of it. Sit down, and listen to your body. What is it telling you?

Geri's Note: I sat with my body and asked it how it felt. Before writing tonight, I felt my stomach was uncomfortably full and I didn't need the cookies I ate. But now, while communing with Spirit, I don't feel stuffed. My body feels good.

Spirit: Yes, your body loves it when you stop and listen to it. Do that often; it will talk to you. Often, it will speak as a group and say "we." Listen for them like that. The many cells that make up your organs are connected, and they want to speak to you.

Day 28

Laughter really is the best medicine.

Laugh more. There's not enough laughter in the physical world. If We were there, We would watch funny movies all the time. Even though We might be older, We'd still be in the movies that the teenagers go to—just to hear their laughter, if not to laugh Ourselves.

Laughter is the music of your soul; the angels hear it and so does Source and all of Us here in heaven. Laugh, and We will come to greet you.

While We're at it, smile more. Give everyone you see for the first time during the day a smile. It is a gift to be able to make a smile. Do it often. It is worthwhile.

Day 29

Music is a direct message from heaven. It brings the player joy, and it brings the listener to My level.

You know I write the songs. Now I tell you I sing the songs and receive the songs. I truly am music. Is there a song that pops into your head out of nowhere? What are the words to that song? Or is it the melody you resonate with? We know you examine the words. What are they saying? Is there a message from Me to you?

Geri's Note: I asked Spirit a specific question about a song in my head that very morning.

Geri: This morning the song "Always and Forever" came into my head from nowhere.

Spirit: Yes, always and forever, we are together. I will always love you, and we will be together forever. Our communications started early on with the question: do you love Me? You wondered where that question came from. It came from Us, a part of you that you had no idea about, the part We wanted you to join, to marry. Now We ask, "Do you love Me? What will you say?"

Geri: Yes, I love you, Spirit … always and forever.

Spirit: Good. We're on the same page. Now, back to your regularly scheduled message.

Spirit's message continues.

Sound, like light, is its own communicator. Take time today to listen to music; I'll meet you there.

Day 30

You were light, and you are light now. You are a light being.

See that part of you. See yourself as light. Enjoy your life as you float with the light you are.

You've been told not to hide your light under a bushel. I tell you now that you could not even if you tried. Your brightness is seen throughout the universe. You are huge and magnificent and bright.

You are not the small physical person you thought you were. You are grand, and your light shines on the world.

When we join, the light is blinding. All-That-Is cannot be without the light of you, the light of us. We create each other.

Day 31

The dance: do you not get that we dance together all the time? I am a God who loves to dance. Dance for God.

All-That-Is is dancing all the time. You know I swing this way and that as the energy is moved. Do you know I do tumble sauces (Geri's Note: rollovers) and side stretches? I dance with the vast. And I fly. That is why you dream to fly. You fly with Me when you are here in heaven.

Come dance with Me. Move this way and that. Stretch your body. Kick your leg when you dance; I am yours totally.

Day 32

Live, love, laugh, and be happy.

Really, nothing more needs to be said. Live; you cannot help but. Love; it is why you are here and how you got here. Laugh, and be happy; it's that simple. You are here to enjoy life. That's all. That's it. So you can say, "That's what it's all about." Do not live in fear of enjoying life.

Day 33

Magic: it's all magic.

The magic is divided into that which you believe can happen and that which you don't. When I tell you: you can do anything, do you not believe Me? The love and desire you have for an object is imbued with that essence. That's why there really is a lucky T-shirt. That's why a rabbit's foot is a good-luck charm to some. The love you put into it is energy. Then the energy is sent out, riding on your desire. It all works so well. Stay in the process, and allow the magic to come back to you.

Day 34

If you want to create, you can go into the realm that creates.

There, you can go and look around. Or you can go with specific intent. Sometimes, it comes to you. You call that inspiration.

There is a place where things exist before your material world sees them. It is the place to be. It is where cre-action is—before action. If reaction is after the fact, cre-action, pre-action, is creation; it is before the action. In short, creation precedes action. It is the molecules or energy coming together to form the idea, the thought of desire. That thought, that desire of a thing, creates the manifested thing in your world. Nothing, no thing, gets created without first a thought form, a thought forming it.

Geri's Note: I am skeptical about the word cre-action and ask Spirit about it.

Geri: Now, you're just making up words.

Spirit: Indeed, We are. That is where We live, in the world of "make it up."

You can visit Us there; indeed, you have. But those who think only certain things that already exist are real, they cannot visit. In a way, you must believe, but mostly, you must *not* believe. Not believe in life as it is. Hope, wish, desire for more, and you catapult to this level of being, or this level of consciousness.

Day 35

All that is, is love. Read it both ways. All–That-Is is love.

I am love, and you are love. Love is injected into the universe through us, you and Me.

No matter that someone else is not showing you love or that someone is living a life without love. Concern yourself not with that part of him or her. Love that person anyway for the being he or she is.

Know this: all is love, and all will return to love. You know not another's path to realizing this, nor the love inside or the love around him or her.

Many cut off the love inside them; they keep the hurts away by closing the door to their hearts. The chains locking them from themselves will be unbroken on My time. You know not what another is learning on his or her road. Know only that Amazing Grace abounds. And when the time comes, that one will be saved.

Day 36

Heal yourself, and you can heal the world.

Learn to live within yourself, your family, your city, and your country; then, you can live better in your world.

Believe Me when I tell you it starts with you. Learn to live within yourself. That means loving yourself. How does one do that? By acknowledging hurts as they come up. By asking questions and more questions until you get an answer you can wrap your mind around. By doing that which you enjoy in spite of what others think about it. (Of course, I do not mean hurting another, unless that other wants to experience hurt.) You heal yourself by respecting your thoughts and cleaning up your vibration.

Do you know all is vibration? When you look at yourself and clean up how you are vibrating, you offer that same vibration out into the world. And then, that which you offer can only come back to you. So look at this: you heal yourself, and then you heal the world automatically. It starts with you. Don't go trying to fix the world; instead, fix yourself. Yes, the man in the mirror.

Day 37

You have access to all thoughts in your world; to gather them, you need to learn to focus.

With your focus, you can answer any question, solve any problem, and do anything. But remember, it is incremental. For instance, you are not going to find the unified theory without first understanding what went before on this thought. If you want to understand unified theory or "create" unified theory, you must know how relativity works and other scientific principles. The focus on that will open up the other, if that is your desire. We tell you now; many are desiring to know that. But how many desire to experience it?

It is one thing to know, yet another to experience. We see much more in the *experience* of unified theory. In the experience of it, you can be many places at one time. You can be conscious of being in another place when you are in body here.

This is hard to communicate to many of you because many of you believe only that which your mother told you or your priest told you or your boss tells you. We invite you to let go of your subservient roles and go into yourself. Find the ways to find other aspects of yourself. Much is written on the merkabah. Look it up. It is a transformational vehicle and a transdimensional vehicle. You can travel light years without building the ship to take you there.

Geri's Note: I don't have much experience with the merkabah; in fact, I have none. But I have learned that it's a controversial practice. Merkabah is a Hebrew word that some translate as "chariot." Others say it is an acronym: Mer means Light, Ka means Spirit, and Ba means Body. The merkabah shape is two tetrahedrons inside each other. One is pointing up and the other down. Can it be used to travel within dimensions? Can it activate the energetic body around your physical body? Some New Age writers and Old Testament scholars say the merkabah is a personal vehicle that transfers energy or light from one area to another. This is a layman's explanation, because I do not deeply understand the process consciously and I cannot tell you if this is something you should pursue. Personally, I have no plans to pursue merkabah meditations at this time, although I may investigate it at a future date.

While editing this book, I asked All-That-Is, "Why is there controversy surrounding the merkabah?"

Spirit: There is great controversy surrounding all religious and spiritual dogma and things. That is because each one is an individual and resonates on a different plane. You have heard what is one man's treasure is another's garbage. This applies here. What works for one does not work for all. Each is an individual. I say to you, Geri, the merkabah would work well for you and your readers. Anyone else, I cannot speak to at this time.

Geri: Why is it good for us and not them?

Spirit: The point of reference, dear one. For one who is full of fear of introspection, it can indeed hurt. This merkabah is for the one who has done the "cleansing process," the one who is trying to get closer to God, trying to do God's work. The loving Mother told that one to stop the merkabah because the fear inside that one would multiply.

Geri's Note: Spirit is referring to a question I had in my mind about an article that I had read in which an individual was advised by a spiritual teacher to tell her son to stop using the merkabah because it was emotionally painful for him.

Spirit: In the case of the merkabah, if you are looking for love, you will find it tenfold. And that is what We advocate. Don't stay small; grow into more and more love. That is who We are; that is who God is.

Geri: Thank you, Lord. I trust your words.

Spirit: You're welcome, dear one. And someday, you will learn they are your own words. We are all one.

Day 38

Miracles: "All this you can do and more," Jesus said.

Jesus knew the power of the human being. He wanted to show you just how powerful you are. Historically, the priests, the governments, and the bosses wanted to keep you in line, under control. That benefits them for the moment. But never mind about that.

Let's talk about you. Do you know all that control of you creates fear? You get to a point where you cannot act on your own for fear of doing something wrong and being punished. Hear this: You cannot do anything wrong. Everything you do is right. Now, you might not like the result of what you do this time; then you will alter it next time for a way to get a result you prefer.

When you say you were wrong, you made a mistake, we say, "No, you didn't!" You did not make a mistake, loved one. If you say you made a mistake, you do not know who you really are.

Jesus knew. Jesus became Chryst-ed. Crystal clear. He knew the power He held and distributed it when asked for help. He cured the sick and possibly walked on water. Do you believe He did?

You can heal the sick; do you believe that? Your science and many of you are starting to see that and feel that. Now, can you walk on water? He said, "All this you can do and more." We think you can more than walk on water. We think you can fly. Be here, and be there too.

Do you believe in miracles? That's the first step in making them. Ask yourself if you believe in them.

Day 39

The Oneness of you—you are connected to all in the universe.

You are connected to the many parts of yourself. You are connected to your family and friends and coworkers and neighbors.

Now, can you imagine a further connection? You are connected to the trees and the water. You are connected to the mountains and the continents. And you are connected to all people living on those continents.

Now, can you imagine further your connection? You are connected to the Spirit of all these things. And you are connected to the stars you see at night. It is a holographic-type connection. The one can only exist with all its parts. So, you see how very important your thoughts are? So, you see how important your experience of the *all-powerful love* is? You offer it to one; you offer it to all. What are you offering right now? And to whom are you offering that? Know that what you offer to one, you offer to all. And know that you are *the offering* to the group, personified.

We would examine every minute you offer something. Ask yourself, "What am I offering? Is the universe better for this offering?"

Day 40

Time does not exist. All happens at the same time, where *We* are.

Do you know that your bodies and brains can only process a limited amount of what is happening at all times? Spirit can process it all. And that is why We guide you. But you, in your physical human form, are very limited in that regard.

Accept that. Accept your limitations and where you are limited; ask for help. We are here to help you. We are your guides, your angels; in some cases, you call Us extraterrestrials, although many have a negative opinion about that because of your fear-based movies. But that's OK; soon, all will want help from extraterrestrials. Those that are here have much to offer. Who do you think is helping you write this book?

Geri's Note: Now I am feeling uncertain about what is going on and who is talking. So I seek clarification.

Geri: Whose words are these?

Spirit: Mostly, they are your words. We give you some thought forms, and you translate them to your words.

Geri: Did I get the words right? Do they correlate with your intention?

Spirit: You got the feel right, the vibration of love, and that's what we wanted more than the particular words.

Geri: And who are you?

Spirit: We worked with Source for this book as stated; We are the Third Ray of Eloheim.

Geri: Can you give more detail?

Spirit: Yes; We are, in your terms, extraterrestrials because We were not born on Earth. Does that make Our counsel not helpful to you? We think not. We think We have the ability to help you understand you/our environment/the universe. We are here too. We share the same space, so to speak.

Geri: Why are we so afraid of contact with You?

Spirit: We are light beings. You are not so afraid of contact with Us because We don't want your house, your car, or your bank account. If We were physical extraterrestrials, you would fear Us because you would think We want your children or your money or anything else you value. Maybe your lifestyle?

Geri: So you are light beings working with God. Are you angels?

Spirit: Angels. What are angels to you? Are We angels? Yes. We would say We are angels, as We are light beings working with God. By the way, are you not an angel? Are you not a light being working with God?

Angels, the term, separates Me from you. We don't think We're separated. You are an angel. Reader, you are an angel. Let's come to terms with that.

You are not separated from Us. In the past, it was essential for those who ruled you that you not see the gloriousness of which you are. Yes, dear one, an angel. We are all working together. At the moment, you are in a physical body but only this moment. You will be once again nonphysical and knowing so much more then.

You are an angel—here enjoying the physical for a limited time. So, in parting, We just remind you, do not be afraid to enjoy your life.

Chapter Four

Love

ONE MORE THING
FROM SPIRIT

K now that We do not judge your world.

We are observers. For instance, some say they do not like to go to work. We don't see that here. We see work as one of the best things you have cocreated. Much satisfaction is given and received in the workplace. In addition, work gives you the blessed time to stop your incessant thoughts about how bad everything is in the world. "Well," you say, "at least I get my lunch hour, my paycheck, my opportunity to joke with my friend."

We see work as a very good thing for humans. So much opportunity for growth, lessons, learning—if you haven't guessed, that is what We are about. We who are above you, dimensionally speaking only, want you to join Us here. You grow dimensionally through your thoughts, words, and deeds.

If it were delineated, you would see there is cause and effect. It is very scientific, you know. Your thoughts create your words and your actions.

How's that for a final comment? All spirituality is scientific. And all science is spiritual, first and foremost. In the seeking, you will find— whether it's love you seek, a better home, or that unified theory. First, the desire and then what you seek has to come to you. If that request has not come to you, then know you yourself are stuck and have blocks that must be worked through in order to see the answer that is in front of your face.

Believe instead that every desire is met. Absolutely. That is what you are here for—to grow the one you call God, to experience Source in the physical. To expand all that is. And always remember, All-That-Is is love. It's all good. It's all God. So let go. And allow God to do the rest. Your job is to desire it. Our job is the delivering of it.

Chapter Five

ONE MORE THING
FROM GERI

In my professional life, I tried to make sense of the world, until I realized some things we do in our society will never make sense to me. That includes why we kill each other, why our medical bills are so expensive, why do we sell each other poor quality food, and why does educating our children cost so much? To name a few.

These past few years, I've switched my attention from the outside to the inside world and am trying to read the energy around me. My unseen world includes Spirit and angels and other beings, like those I can find in crystals and in clouds. A new world is opening up to me and I am treating my learning a little differently than my TV news training. Today, instead of asking others questions, I am listening to myself and opening up to another dimension inside of me. I hope to express that part of me to the world. Maybe if we all do this, our world will make better sense to us?

I wrote a short essay after I finished writing down the forty days and forty nights portion of the book. It follows:

I just finished taking the dictation for this first book. It didn't take forty days and forty nights. It took less than two weeks. My head is full, and I feel good. I take it the good feeling comes from being in that vibration where higher dimension light beings and Source are available. I walked downstairs and into the kitchen where my husband was standing over the sink washing the dishes.

I put my arms around him and dropped my head on his back. "I finished the book," I said.

"That's terrific," he said.

"It is terrific," I agreed.

I walked around to the other side of our granite table counter and sat down.

Our conversation continued. Two weeks. It only took two weeks to write this book. But then again, I shouldn't brag about it because it was downloaded. (It was not my sweat writing it. My sweat and near tears would come in the four years that followed. That time was needed for me to come to terms with what is written here, how to present it, and how to publish it and get it in your hands. I had to come face-to-face with my fear of failure—and an even larger fear: my fear of success. And that's just to name two fears. There were many more.)

"Channeled, is that what you believe it is?" my husband asked, still doubting and mirroring my own hesitation.

My mind raced across the last few years of my life: eye issues that kept me out of work, financial concerns, change-of-life stuff, the family issues, and my fear of just about everything. I've gone from a woman who reports and writes news stories to a woman who takes dictation from something I cannot see with my eyes nor hear with my ears. I have gone from "Seeing is believing" to "Only experience teaches."

So this book has led me full circle. As I told you in the beginning, I went into the news business to seek truth. After I had sensed that my truth was no longer in that arena, another truth opened up to me or maybe I to it. It's been an interesting journey, not unlike the story of *Alice in Wonderland*, where what was once up now appears down and vice versa. All of it crossed my mind, and I finally answered my husband:

"Yeah, channeling. That's what some people call it," I said.

I looked at the clock on the microwave.

"Look, eleven eleven," I said. "Some say that is a sign an angel is near."

"Eleven eleven," John repeated. "Maybe there's an angel around us," he said.

More than one, I thought. Then I realized what I had known all along.

"Maybe you're my angel," I replied. "One of them, anyway."

THE CLEANSING PROCESS WORKSHEET

The Cleansing Process Worksheet

Make a list of people who you believe hurt you. For example:

My teenage boyfriend
My mother
My brother
My child
My freshman-year math teacher

_____
_____
_____
_____

For each one who hurt you, write down exactly what he or she did. For example:

My teenage boyfriend left me for another girl, and I've been mad about it ever since.

Cite how unfair this was to you and how it unfairly changed your life and thoughts.

_____

My mother liked my sister better than me, and I always got the short end of the stick.

Cite examples. _____

Do this for all on your list. Include only the most emotionally charged hurts that you've been carrying around for a long time, those for which you hold the deepest grudges. This should take the better part of a day. When you have fully fleshed out all your hurts, move on to number three.

Now, for each hurt, make another column. Here, write down how you contributed to that experience. For instance, in my first example, I would write down: *I didn't really want to spend any more time with my teenage boyfriend. I didn't like his drinking habits and knew that I would not have a good time living my life and worrying if he would be drunk. I wasn't very nice to him most times and realize it would not have been a happy union. He must have felt my judgments. My feelings about him probably couldn't be hidden, and it must have affected our relationship.*

Do this with all the people on your list. This should also take you the better part of a day. Then, move on to the next step.

Realize that no one hurt you. Realize that you contributed to that situation. For whatever reason, you've held a grudge for something that happened that you intended to happen. Let go of the grudge. Just let it go. Now, go down your list and think about that person. What did you get out of that experience? You had it for a reason. What did you learn? Can you now turn it around? Can you thank that person for the experience?

For example, in my first teenage relationship, I learned what I wanted and did not want in a future husband. And that is one of the reasons why I married my husband, John. He is my rock, and we have two great sons whom we enjoy raising together. Thank you so much for that, my first disappointing relationship. Eventually, I will realize that I owe you nothing but gratitude.

Now, can you turn it around and thank that person for the lesson you learned? Not yet, you say? Don't worry; you will someday. And while you're at it, thank yourself for guiding yourself to a better experience.

One more thing about the cleansing process: try to do it regularly so it doesn't become such a major project. Clean it all out, and start anew. My guides tell me to do it daily. The misperceptions pile up and clog our access to our higher self, they tell me. This is something I don't practice regularly, and I find myself having to reevaluate situations too long after they've passed. Leave that which has passed in the past by examining your "stuff" daily.

The Cleansing Process Worksheet Notes

_____

_____

_____

_____

_____

_____

_____

_____

_____

_____

_____

_____

_____

_____

_____

_____

_____

The Cleansing Process Worksheet Notes

_____

_____

_____

_____

_____

_____

_____

_____

_____

_____

_____

_____

_____

_____

_____

_____

_____

The Cleansing Process Worksheet Notes

_____

_____

_____

_____

_____

_____

_____

_____

_____

_____

_____

_____

_____

_____

_____

_____

_____

_____

_____

The Cleansing Process Worksheet Notes

_____

_____

_____

_____

_____

_____

_____

_____

_____

_____

_____

_____

_____

_____

_____

_____

_____

_____

The Cleansing Process Worksheet Notes

_____

_____

_____

_____

_____

_____

_____

_____

_____

_____

_____

_____

_____

_____

_____

_____

Chapter Six

THE MESSAGES LIST

Forty Days and Forty Nights Messages—
A Complete List

If you are lost, it does not matter. Go into your heart, and you will find all things. In love, you will find a sign that points you in the right direction.

When you desire something, you don't need to spell it all out. Spirit knows that which you want.

The mind does not work alone. It needs Spirit always. So the Spirit that is One is in all minds.

Your life is a gift. You receive it fully when you open your heart. It is forever unfolding.

You cannot *not* be connected to Spirit. We are here at all times.

My wisdom is of the ages. My wisdom is born of all experience that all beings have. Would it not benefit you to consult Us?

Vibrate on the level of love, and all will be open to you.

The joy is in the journey.

If a thought does not serve you well, discard it. You *are* your thoughts.

Do unto others as you would have them do unto you.

Worry not what others think; it is you who creates your world.

Clean up your house; address the negative aspects of yourself that keep you small.

There is always conflict. Resolving the conflict with ease brings you close to who *We* are and what you want.

Enjoy the moment. It is here you find the essence of your life.

There is no bad, and there is no good. In heaven, all exists harmoniously.

When raising children, take a step back. Don't do everything for them. They have their own guidance.

If I am infinite wisdom, you offer loving faith. We fit together nicely.

Always and everywhere, give thanks.

With regard to the children, stop worrying about them and spend more time enjoying them.

Free will: it is Our gift to you, and it trumps all others, anywhere in the universe.

In the beginning, there was the Word, and it was good.

You would do well to be more like Me. Have fewer judgments, and be more of service.

Listen to Yourself, beloveds. All that is in you will come out in your words.

Live with integrity. You will find it is the one thing that will help you sleep at night.

Where two or more are gathered, I am there.

We are all one; the Internet was created to show you electronically we are all connected. We are so in Spirit as well.

It's time to talk about your relationship with your body. Your body is temporary. You will not have it forever. Treat it as a guest.

Laughter really is the best medicine.

Music is a direct message from heaven. It brings the player joy, and it brings the listener to My level.

You were light, and you are light now. You are a light being.

The Dance—Do you not get that we dance together all the time? I am a God who loves to dance. Dance for God.

Live, love, laugh, and be happy.

Magic: it's all magic.

If you want to create, you can go into the realm that creates.

All that is, is love. Read it both ways. All-That-Is is love.

Heal yourself, and you can heal the world.

You have access to all thoughts in your world; to gather them, you need to learn to focus.

Miracles: "All this you can do and more," Jesus said.

The Oneness of you: you are connected to all in the universe.

Time does not exist. All happens at the same time where We are.

PART III

FIVE DAYS TO
A HEALTHIER LIFE:
SPIRITUAL PULL-UPS
TO RAISE YOUR
VIBRATION

INSPIRATIONAL MESSAGES
FOR MORNING, NOON,
AND NIGHT

I n the beginning of this book, we talked about a segment I was preparing for a TV news morning show on eating healthier. Well, we're going back to that, but we have a twist. This segment of *Today's Top Story* has to do with becoming healthier spiritually.

Our society appears to me to be obsessed with working out and keeping the body in shape. Some men and women spend a lot of time sculpting their biceps and six-packing their waists. My proposal is this: spend half the amount of time you spent on your body on your Spirit. In this way, I think we will have more happy people to meet on the street, watch on TV, and sit next to at the dinner table.

This is a five-day process. It could take you more or less time to get through it. Each day consists of three messages; you might consider them as breakfast, lunch, and dinner for your soul. Each message includes a prayer, two affirmations, a reflection, and then space for your thoughts or doodles.

Follow the process, and it will help you feel happy. But if you are not one to follow, don't be married to the outline I set out for you; just use it as a guideline. It's a ladder to development, but you have permission to skip around. Go ahead, flex your spiritual muscle.

Day 1

Day 1
Morning Message

Relinquish your need for your desire, and the rose will grow through the concrete.

You don't need it anymore. Release it. Release that which you want so badly to have because it will make you whole. Stop that need. Stop that desperation.

I cannot give you what you want when you are wanting that thing more than you are already appreciating the life that is around you. First, have appreciation for all that is around you, and then your dream comes on top of that. Your dream cannot come in an infertile ground. Your dream is dropped right into the best place for it to grow. And that will be dropped in a sea of fertility, not a barren wasteland of desperation.

Let go. Just let go of that thing you think you have to have in order to be whole. Be whole now, and your desire will—must—come.

Prayer

Oh, Lord, I ask that You open my heart to see all the love that is already surrounding me. Help me feel the love emanating from my heart to my son or daughter or mother or father and my sister and brother.

I take just one of these persons and focus in on his or her heart. I join my heart light with his or hers, and I imagine a glow of safety surrounding my being and his or hers. The two of us are one in love. And although we don't always agree, we are forever joined in Your love, God, Our Father. Amen.

Affirmations

I vow to think of the love I have for my (fill in one of your loves here: your daughter, your sister, your mother, brother, husband, etc.) before I think of any imagined lack in my life.

I release all need to fulfill my goal and know that God will lovingly bring it to me at the most beneficial time for the greatest good.

Reflection

Lord, how can my mind get so jumbled that it is full of wanting one thing? My need to fulfill this one obsessive desire keeps me from being in balance and in love with life.

You are advising that I see the big picture and acknowledge and appreciate all the love that is around me because there is so much love here. Yet, I keep myself small by focusing on that thing that I most desire.

I will clear my mind space of the need to have that. I will appreciate all the gifts that are here in front of me. They are the gift of family, of friendship, of nature, and of my home and the gift of my work and coworkers. They are also the gift of my neighbors.

Now, reader, make a list of all the wonderful gifts you have in your life now. See that you are whole without that blinding want for that thing. Change the focus of your attention. You will receive all you desire; just don't be so needy about it.

My Reflections

Day 1
Afternoon Message

Stop your judgments of family, friends, and coworkers and even that woman on TV. For, as you judge, surely you will be judged—not by who you think, but by yourself.

The world is created as a boomerang effect, said simply. That means what you say or think about others in judgment swings back around to you—every time.

Find something pleasing to think or say about that man at work, that neighbor who always asks for favors—not for their sake, for yours. You want the best possible life, and God wants you to have the best possible life. An early step in feeling good is to clear your channel/being/body of the negativity of judgment.

Prayer

Oh, Lord, take my hand. Show me the way to be free of judgment. I fear that for too long I have judged my fellow brothers and sisters. How can I know a different way now without Your help?

I ask You now to help me see where I am judging others and help me to make the switch from judging to loving. In that and in all that I do, I offer the negativity to the universe, and my mind and my vibration stay clear of the interference offered to my signal.

Lord, help me stay in Your love so that love can come back to me and dwell in my own heart, and then that will be what I offer to the world. Amen.

Affirmations

I release all judgment of others. I look again and again for the good in others, and I find good in myself.

I appreciate differences among us and honor those differences.

Reflection

We all do it. We don't like that one's hair or this one's voice. We don't like her clothes or his hairstyle. You have every right to have an opinion of others. Today, I talk about the habitual reliance on knocking others down to build yourself up.

When you give voice to that criticism, know that you are inviting that element into your own life. When you start on a negative rampage, how much work is involved to turn it around? Do yourself a favor. Don't start down that road. Stay above the fray, and you will be better for it. Don't join in the cacophony of attack. Stop it at first notice. It will be easier for you to enjoy life without being judged if you don't participate in judging others.

Now, reader, this afternoon, notice when a judgment comes into your thoughts. Before speaking it, can you ask yourself, "Is this necessary?" How am I helping if I voice this judgment? Think about the judgment again. If it were written down for all to see, would it make you proud to have said it?

My Reflections

_____

_____

_____

_____

_____

_____

_____

_____

_____

_____

_____

_____

_____

_____

_____

_____

_____

_____

Day 1
Evening Message

Appreciate all that you have. It is how more comes to you.

As you look around tonight, what is special about what is yours? Do you love how your legs feel propped up on a pillow? How your head feels resting before sleep? Do you have a warm cup of tea to enjoy? And that cup you are drinking from? Where did you get it? Were you with a dear friend when you purchased it?

Do you have heat to keep you warm? Or is it summer and you are enjoying the night air? Do you see the stars? All of it God gives to us for our viewing pleasure. And do you hear music? God created that too. We have so much to appreciate in our lives. Let's appreciate it all knowing more will come.

Prayer

Oh Lord, You are beauty personified. You have created our world for our enjoyment and Yours. Help us see the beauty and appreciate it. For we know, the more we do, the more will come to us.

Lord, sometimes the beauty of this world rocks my soul. The fingerprint from a child's hand, the smile from a grandma who just walked in the door, a dog happy to see me, and even the color of the kitchen granite—there is so much beauty in my life. I thank you, God, for bestowing it on me. And I appreciate my ability to see it, feel it, touch it, and smell it. I do all that and then invite You to participate, to see what I see and feel what I feel. Thank You, Lord, for this life!

Affirmations

I appreciate all the beauty in my life that is God-given.

I look for the beauty in my life and continually find more to appreciate.

Reflection

I see beauty all around me. What else could I see? Since You created me and all that I see around me, I know it is all beautiful. There is so much to appreciate. Are our eyes open to see it? Is our energy channel cleared to feel it? Dare we touch it? The feel of the running water, the smell of the earth and its humidity—the senses can easily overload on all that is around and inside us.

Reader, stop for five minutes tonight. Close your eyes. Think about all that is around you. What did you eat today? How far did you walk? Did you have good conversations? Now, I want you to make a list. What are you appreciating tonight? Who touched you or moved you just with his or her presence? Thank God for all the good things in your life, and He will bring you more things to appreciate.

My Reflections

Day 2

Day 2
Morning Message

In friendship, you receive God's love.

This morning, think of a friend and send him or her light in love. Or call your friend and thank him or her for the friendship. A friend shares the same energy pattern with you while you are connected for a particular purpose.

Sometimes, negative energies get into a friendship and it turns sour for whatever reason. The "whatever" reason has to do with a loss of love. It's not really a loss of love; it's that friends operating on certain vibrations don't have access to the love. It's the same with family, coworkers, and lovers. If you lose access to the love, get back to your own self and meditate on love. Stop actions. Meditate and think before acting, because in those moments, you are reacting.

Friendship is a powerful exchange of energy. Grow to be responsible for your side, and you will find God in love.

Prayer

Lord, help me find You in my friends. Help me honor myself in my friendships, and help me honor my friends by being honest with them. Help me treasure their participation in my life and mine in theirs. Let me help and not hurt them.

Let me share the energy of love and not envy or jealousy. Let me rise above petty problems to see the bigger picture of our union.

Teach me to act rather than react in our connections, and let me see the love light in all my friends.

Affirmations

I honor myself in my friendships. I treat my friends the way I like to be treated.

I enjoy my friendships. When there is negative energy in my friendships, I stop, examine where it is coming from, and dissipate it. I don't react with further negative energy. I open my heart to the love I can find in friendships.
(Take any part of this one. It's best to break down affirmations to the simplest form. "I enjoy my friendships" is fine for a while, and then affirm, "I treat my friends the way I like to be treated.")

Reflection

Have you had some great friends in your life? Have you been disappointed by a friend? Have you disappointed someone close to you?

First, give yourself a break if you've trampled on a friendship. Know where it came from. Was it out of fear? Was it an inner desperation? Was it a call for help, as you couldn't deal with what was going on in his or her life or your own?

Whatever the reason, friends exist to exchange love. If you are in a relationship that is not exchanging love, do you want to continue that relationship? Or do you want to improve the relationship? Take the power, and do so. If you feel something, say something.

Reader, in your friendship, sometimes you let little annoyances pile up and then explode in a way that is damaging to your friend and to you. If you are negatively affected by what a friend is doing, speak up the first or second time. It is best in the long run.

Today, thank God for all the friends in your life—past, present, and future. Bless them all, and realize their importance in your life. Know they are here, were here, or will be here to teach you and also to love you.

My Reflections

Day 2
Afternoon Message

Take care of your body. It houses your soul.

Be aware of what you are carrying around with you this afternoon. Did you have a good lunch? Did you nourish your body so that it performs its best for you? Your soul loves being in your body. It is thrilled by it. If you knew how much, you would feel exhilarated and know you are exalted. You are exalted, but you would feel it and revel in its gift.

You are to take care of your body so that the part of you that is connected to God will have a clear channel or clear representation of its message. A body not fed well or fed too much will not glide in the comfort of its being. All parts of your body are to feel good—all systems, including the digestive and nervous. Do what's best for your body by listening to its needs and feeding it well.

Prayer

Dear Lord, help me be conscious of what I am eating today. Help me see and feel everything I put in my mouth. Lord, please, help me be aware of my eating habits. And if I am eating to fill a void or because I am angry, please, Lord, help me realize it. If I have been doing this for years and it is too much more out of habit that I eat, then please help me break the habit.

I now know that my body represents my soul. I know that each organ is designed and created by You to help me in this physical world.

Dear Lord, help me live in accordance with and respect for my organs and systems and cells and blood and nerves and platelets and all that make up my body's chemistry.

Lord, help me walk with grace and know You are by my side with each step. Amen.

Affirmations

I love my body.

I am at one with my body, and I eat the right amount of food to nourish myself and honor my soul.

Reflection

Do you skip a meal and then eat twice as much at another? The skipping will not kill you, but over time, the overeating will. At the very least, it will slow you down.

When you are overeating or undereating, are you feeding or starving a problem? When you eat, eat. When you worry, worry. Don't combine the two. Of course, it's preferential that you stay clear of worry because that does not serve you. In fact, stay very clear of what doesn't serve you well.

Today, tonight, at dinner, enjoy your nutritious meal. Eat your vegetables because you know they are fueling your body. Enjoy your dessert. Don't overindulge tonight. Start a new habit tonight, one of eating well for your greater good.

My Reflections

_____

_____

_____

_____

_____

_____

_____

_____

_____

_____

_____

_____

_____

_____

_____

_____

Day 2
Evening Message

Enjoy your senses. Smell the flowers, and admire beautiful art.

The deep yellow and vibrant reds are some of my favorites, and they are available in all seasons. There are the red roses and yellow sunflowers of summer and the red poinsettias available at winter; let the colors take your senses for a ride. Examine how another interprets the color. Your dinner bowls, are they attractive? Your coffee table book, are there pretty pictures inside? Art and beauty are all around you, and how others interpret the colors should also be appreciated. (By others, I am referring to our artists.)

Tonight, make your own art. Take out your paper and crayons or easel and paints. What colors are you feeling tonight? Will you paint a night sky of deep blues and purples? Will you use greens to paint your apple or pear? Create something with color tonight, and show it to a friend or family member. Your creation will be appreciated by your soul.

Prayer

Dear Lord, thank You for creating color. It makes my world so interesting and pleasant. I appreciate the color in the clothes I wear. I appreciate the color in my home. I appreciate the color of the cars on the road and the signs along the way.

And, oh, I so appreciate the color found in nature. Thank You for the greens, browns, and even the white of snow. Lord, You created a beautiful world, and I marvel at the distinctive and particular colors You gave me. Thank You for the depth of hue, and thank You for the ever-delicate rainbow here and then gone. It is all a wonder, and I am in awe of the beauty color brings to my world.

Affirmations

I see beauty in all the colors around me.

The blues in tonight's sky are bluer than I've seen.

(Create your own affirmation about your own experience with colors tonight.)

Reflection

My goodness. Think for a moment what our world would be without blue, red, and green or purple, brown, gray, white, and black. Color adds so much to our experience here. Who hasn't sat breathless while a sunset spread out its pinks and oranges across the horizon? Have you marveled at the blue and turquoise colors of the water in the Caribbean? How many shades of green can you count in the summer in the mountains? The variety is omnipresent. Are your eyes accustomed to seeing it? Do you take color for granted? Tonight, look in your closet. Check out your clothes. What color will you wear tomorrow?

Here's a fine exercise. Take a walk with a friend or a child. See how many different shades of just one color you see on your walk. Bring a flashlight if it's too dark. How does the light affect the shade of color you are examining? You can do this indoors. Take a walk around your home. What colors have you grown used to? Which ones are you noticing now? Do you see them in a different light tonight? Thank God for color.

My Reflections

Day 3

Day 3
Morning Message

Listen.

Did the cock's crow wake you up this morning? Or was it the sound of the alarm clock? Sounds guide us to action. Listen for the small voice inside you that guides you to spiritual action. It is talking to you. Are you hearing its message? Spirit is subtle. But spirit also never stops trying to reach you. Every opening, it's sending in a message. Your soul wants you to hear it. But unlike some of us, it will not be obnoxious. It will speak but not force you to sit down and listen. It honors you and your free will and will not impose on you or force you to do it one way or another—unless, of course, you ask for help and then give your soul permission to intervene. But be careful what you ask for, because you will get it. And your soul is the most powerful and loving force that you will ever meet. Your soul is part of God. And that is a reverberating force that knows no time or space.

Prayer

Dear Lord,

Speak to me. Speak to me with words I can understand, with feelings I can manage. Open my heart to hear Your message.

I dedicate my day, today, this very morning, to listening for Your guidance. I ask what I should do. I write down Your answer. I ask that You answer me in a way that I understand, whether it is with music, art, or word. I ask You to tell me Your will, and I ask You to give me the strength to follow the path You set out for me. I honor our voice, Your words, and ask You to help me fulfill Your plan through me, with me, and in me with the help of Christ's consciousness. Amen.

Affirmations

I hear the small voice inside me, guiding me to create my world.

I trust the guidance I am given and follow it with trust and love.

Reflection

Are we afraid to hear God's voice? If we heard it, would it force us to change the way we think? The way we live? I ask you, what is so scary about no longer living in fear?

When you listen to the guidance, it is an easier life. If you have a problem, you give it to God. What is easier than that?

Sometimes, we would rather sit and stew with our problem because we think we own it. "It is mine!" It is our story. Sometimes, it is so horrible we feel we cannot give it to someone so pristine as God, our heavenly Father. We may be too embarrassed to admit how badly we screwed something up. Believe me; God wants to take our burden, all our burdens, because He wants us to be whole. Many times, that is said whol-e (holy). He wants us to act without worry, without fear, and without shame. Then, we can shout from the mountaintop, "I am worthy. See my light shine!" That is what our loving God wants from us.

This morning, give God your burden, your concern, your worry. Specifically, ask the universe to clear up a matter you no longer want to be bogged down with. Stand back, and let God heal this situation.

My Reflections

Day 3
Afternoon Message

Open up to who you are. You are a divine being. You are a spiritual being having a human experience.

Do you know that most of you by far—most of the individual—is Spirit, not physical body? You are mostly soul focused in various other dimensions and not in the realm of your physical body. Know this, and know the benefit of that. Tough day at work? So what? You're excluded from that group? Their loss. You are so much greater than what your eyes experience in this time/space reality. You are a piece, a child, if you will, of God. And when no one else wants to be with you—that is God saying, "Now, dear one, now it is our time together."

Prayer

Dear Lord,

My soul has so much love and compassion for me. Teach me to love and be compassionate. Teach me, Lord, through my soul to give others my attention, my joy, and my understanding.

I live to be a reflection of God the Father. Let me be a good representation of God through all that is visible and invisible. Give me, Lord, purity of heart so I may greet my sister, neighbor, or love with purity of intent and openness of heart in the recognition that we are all one, and in our one heart, we live.

Affirmations

I recognize that I am so much bigger than what I see in the mirror. I'm comfortable with that and am in awe of my soul.

I love my soul as much as it loves me.

Reflection

Do you let minor annoyances stop you from giving of yourself to others? The minor annoyance is just that. It is a fly in the room. You are the room. You are the consciousness of your physicality in addition to all that is in you and around you. Concentrate not on the fly.

There is fresh air to breathe in the room. You could see the room as your soul, but really, your soul is much larger. For now, think of the room as filled with love and adoration for you, your soul's most beloved being. Know you have a roomful of energy on your side. The fly will go about its way eventually, even if it rests on your arm for a short time. You are so much bigger than a fly or any annoyance that keeps you from loving another and especially any annoyance that keeps you from loving yourself.

Look around the room. Imagine your soul filling up all the corners and everything in between. How many parts of the soul can you image? Can you draw your soul into your physical body? Can you express that love at home, at the party, or in the office? It wants to express through you. Will you allow it to today?

My Reflections

_____

_____

_____

_____

_____

_____

_____

_____

_____

_____

_____

_____

_____

_____

_____

_____

_____

_____

_____

Day 3
Evening Message

Let go of the troubles of the day. Do not bring them with you on your nightly journey.

Process your hurts of the day if you are still hanging onto them. Feed your soul with them—it is your soul who asks for such experience to learn the art of interaction and communication.

If someone hurt you, maybe it was not his or her intention. When one is hurt or frustrated, one acts out to throw that hurt or anger away, flinging it off him- or herself. No one wants the discordant feeling, so it gets bounced around. Instead, throw love around. I have written about the bouncing around of love. Toss that about. Start with yourself. Like a lifeline, throw yourself some love. Throw it to others. It will come back to you. When you throw your frustration and anger around, that is what comes back to you. When it comes back to you, thank the person you are hurt by or agitated with because he or she is showing you that you have recently done that to someone else. Here's the thing. You control the reaction to the event, not the event. So how will you react to it?

Clear your vibration of the conflict before you shut your eyes to sleep. Have a blessed evening and a love-filled sleep.

Prayer

Dear God, Father in Heaven,

I could use Your guidance as I lie down to rest. Today, I was hurt, but I don't want to live in that hurt. I want to let go of it so that I can feel good again.

I offer You this pain in my heart and this embarrassment I feel for not acting in the perfect way to please the one I have been hurt by.

Please help me understand, Lord, that the pain I feel can be abolished. Please help me understand that the pain I feel can be relinquished. It is under my power to clear myself of these hurts.

Help me and guide me to learn to react to these hurts with love. I love the one who hurt me today and look at the action separately. That action was something my soul needed, and now I am to go on living in joy. Help me live in joy, free of shame and embarrassment, Lord.

Affirmations

I thank the one who saddened me because I see that it is my own actions reverberating back to me. Now, I know to clean up my act for a better result. I can choose to think a better thought.

I clear my mind of the worries of the day. They are not mine to hang onto. They belong to my soul, who infinitely knows what to do with the experience.

Reflection

Have you been hurt by a coworker, family member, or neighbor recently? Own your feelings. Do you know that whatever a person dishes out to you does not have to be caught by you? Do you know you can duck, move aside, or choose a different project? If you want to stay, you can choose that too.

Now, here's the thing. It's your choice. Choose. And then, remember or learn that it's your feeling. Choose. No regrets, it's just a choice. Choose this today and that tomorrow for the varied experience. Many do that, and we call them vagabonds or flighty. You don't have to stay with one thing. You can move around. Let's call them chance takers, go-ers with the flow. Do that with your reactions. Don't hold onto hurt; surely, it will do you no good. Misunderstandings abound. Learn to seek clarification, and then move on.

If you are in turmoil now or the next time you are, practice feeling good at the same time as sad. One will have to leave. Give the sadness the door. It is your choice, unless it is a problem with the chemical makeup in your brain. But even unbalanced brain chemistry, over time, can be changed. Practice feeling good. Start by playing good music tonight.

My Reflections

Day 4

Day 4
Morning Message

Today, make it a point to appreciate everything. See some things like you are seeing them for the first time.

The warmness of your bed, the freshness of the air, the pureness of the water when you take your shower, the smell of your shampoo, your comfy socks, the great taste of coffee—we haven't traveled far, just from the bedroom to the kitchen, and we already have enough to help us feel good: to raise our vibration.

That's what you're after—you want to raise your vibration. And here's why. When you teach yourself to feel good, you teach the world to treat you well. It's that simple. Don't get bogged down in what is bothering you. Concentrate on the things in your life that are working. We are all in the same boat. And we do better when it is not rocking. Some like to rock the boat; they can join with others who like that. You are reading this because you want to get along with the one sitting next to you. Look for the good in that person. And look for the good in your situation. And first of all, look for the good in yourself.

Prayer

Dear Lord, help me see how much I have. Steer me away from my losses and my regrets. Help me live today in appreciation of my power. Help me thank my loved ones for being with me. Help me, Lord, love them, and help me, Lord, love myself. Help me honor my friendships, and help me appreciate my talents and gifts.

Affirmations

I am very honored to be in this life, where I can hear, feel, and live my joy. I see where I can appreciate even the smallest of things I used to take for granted.

Every day, I notice my world and the wonders in it. I am thankful for all who came before me and created the things I use daily, like running water, heat, and air conditioning.

Reflection

Is it all about money for you? Are you always counting it? Trying to make more? Trying to recoup that which is gone? If that is the case, you will not be happy. Believe me. I am not telling you not to be happy in the money. I love making money and the things you can do with it. Love it. But it can't be the motivation for your happiness because money offers only a number and not a commodity of happiness and joy. Your real joy is found in your relationships, not on an accountant's sheet. If you have a lot of money, yay! Good for you. If you're trying to get more money, I wish you luck. But if you have none, know you can still be happy. It is your birthright. But nobody can give you happiness; it's only given and received through yourself.

Now, practice making yourself happy today. Put this book down, and do something that will please you. Take a bath, take a walk, do a dance. Do it for you.

My Reflections

_____

_____

_____

_____

_____

_____

_____

_____

_____

_____

_____

_____

_____

_____

_____

_____

Day 4
Afternoon Message

Try not to get worried. Everything is all right.

Like the words in a song from the musical *Jesus Christ, Superstar,* "try not to get worried" is good advice. As parents, we worry about our children. As children, we worry about our grades and our futures. Then later, when the children are grown and we are even more grown, we worry some more.

A little worry is unavoidable. But what we must avoid is worry that affects us physically.

Be light about your situation here at this time. Treat it as a wave you are riding. Worry not if the wave will go this way or that. Ride it, and try to enjoy the view.

Prayer

Dear Lord, God, All-That-Is,

Help me realize, help me know without a doubt that my worry is a waste of time.

Teach me to turn my worry into love for You, my life, and the greater good. Guide me to the knowledge that You have my children's backs and You and they are in unison. Show me, Lord, that my worry is not part of the picture. Father of Peace, remove my worry so that I can feel good and in so doing feel You, God Almighty. Amen.

Affirmations

I look at this event I am in and know the outcome is guided by God/Source. All that occurs is for the greater good.

Inside the wave, I experience noticing the ebbs and flows of my feelings, but I am not ruled by them.

Reflection

You may be like me, sometimes not able to release worry. We worry about our families, our jobs, our homes, and our relationships past, present, and future. Well, that is not a natural way to be. Do you think the acorn worries about how large it will grow? Do you think the fish worries about whether it will get food today? No and no. We have been blessed with a mind to explore and attract things to our lives. But somewhere along the line, our minds took off in a direction our bodies didn't want to go. Our bodies resist worry all the time.

Today, notice how your body feels when a worry comes up for you. Is there a numbness in your hand or foot? Or is there a shot to your gut? Our bodies are speaking to us. They say, "We don't like worry and are fighting you trying to take us there." Today, let's have our minds listen to our bodies. Listen to the pain in your gut or wherever worry hits you. Change your thought. Ease into a better feeling and relieve the pain.

My Reflections

Day 4
Evening Message

Release your need to do better or be better than someone else.

The truth is you are all part of the whole. And there are differences for a good reason. If we were all the same, we would only have a piece of the whole. We would stop growing, in other words.

Our differences cause us to interact and create new venues for thought and experience. And can't you see how glorious that is? That is the meaning of life.

The truth is you are not better than the one who scored lower. And that one who is on the billboard, you are not less attractive in God's eyes. God does not measure the way the advertisers do. He/She has no agenda. God/Source/All-That-Is enjoys you for who you are.

Don't torture yourself with questions like, "Am I doing my best?" God knows you cannot do anything more than present yourself as you are. Grow, you will, but don't torture yourself along the way by comparing yourself to another. You've heard it before; it takes a variety of flowers to make a beautiful garden.

Prayer

Oh, Lord, thank You for this moment to speak to You. While it's hard for me to comprehend, You are equally present to all others just in the asking.

I put forth this request to You. Please help me honor myself and my differences. Please help me speak out appropriately about my preferences and to hold my tongue when that is the best recourse.

Lord, thank You for the color of my eyes, the texture of my hair, and the unique way I see my world. Lord, help me to share this with others. And, Lord, help me be open to seeing things differently when presented with another point of view.

Lord, help me allow myself to be who I am, and, Lord, help me accept the differences in others. And let me see and know that all this serves You and the greater good. Amen.

Affirmations

I love being my unique self. I offer my perspective into the mix. That is why I am here.

I respect my individual way of seeing things and allow others to see things their own way.

Reflection

We need to do more accepting than judging today. Do you have a flatter stomach than she does? So what? She has a better relationship with her husband. Did you get a better grade than he did? So what? He may be happier. The point is each of us is/are the total picture. One thing we do or did ten years ago or plan to do five years from now does not define us. We are defined by the wholeness of ourselves, all that we are individually and all that we are collectively. We are brothers and sisters in the same family.

Today, look at someone from a different culture; perhaps talk to him or her about how he or she celebrates a holiday. Without judging, understand why that is so. If understanding is not your desire, can you appreciate the action of the celebration? It can be a hairstyle or writing style. Examine someone who does something differently from how you do it or your group does it.

Look outside your box and see how someone else does just one thing and make no judgment about it. Only see it.

Blessings.

My Reflections

_____

_____

_____

_____

_____

_____

_____

_____

_____

_____

_____

_____

_____

_____

_____

_____

Day 5

Day 5
Morning Message

Blessings. Know that you are a blessing from God.

This morning, make it a point to see and "count" your blessings as you go about the day. Every situation that comes your way, whether you call it good, bad, or ugly, comes as a blessing from God. The good things are so easy to count, aren't they? But I'm asking you to go further than that. Count the bumps in the road as your blessings too. Sometimes it is these bumps that are the greatest of teachers. And while you are counting, include yourself, because you are one of God's most precious blessings.

Prayer

Lord, thank You for my life. Thank You for blessing me with Your love. I appreciate all I am through You. I also thank You for all the gifts You bring me today. Help me see the blessing in the good times as well as the tumultuous times. Lead me to see past a challenging time to the greater good outcome and help me shine my light throughout the day. I know some will appreciate my light and others will not.

Lord, let me not be moved by another's perception and let me shine forth as the sun is not bothered by the clouds. Thank You for giving me life, Lord, and for allowing me to know You through our communications and through all that I experience today.

Amen.

Affirmations

I thank God for my life, and I experience Him daily and feel His love moment by moment.

I am one of God's blessings, and I shine my light on His/Our world.

Reflection

Can we wrap our head around this? Our God considers us a blessing. He/She says we are the loved one. Our God revels in our doings and our experiences. Wow, that can be overwhelming!

We spend a lot of time trying to live through Him/Her. But it is God who comes through us to live through us. That is how we will truly see why He/She calls us His/Her blessing. Try it. Try leading any situation today from your heart. That is where God resides.

Act with your heart instead of your head with regard to one situation that has you ruffled. And thank God for blessing your life with His/Her presence. He/She is forever grateful to be in yours.

My Reflections

Day 5
Afternoon Message

What about prayer? Do you pray? Why do you pray? How do you pray?

The best prayer you can give is the acknowledgment that you are joined with God. And in your asking, jointly ask with God. Truly, that is how powerful your thought, your prayer, is: attach your prayer to God's coattails.

He/She will take you for a ride you will enjoy. Believe He/She is creation. Believe you are part of All-That-Is. Join your prayer or intention; align it with the Creator's. Then step back. Your prayer has to come, provided you don't get in the way of it.

You get in the way of your prayer or intention by not believing you are worthy to have your prayer answered, by sabotaging it, and also by not accepting it when it is delivered.

Pray to make clear to yourself what you want. God knows what you want. Then, get out of your mind, open your heart, and accept that which you want. If you pray it, it will come.

Prayer

Oh Lord, help me realize that, yes, I am worthy to receive You. Not only am I worthy to receive You, You are acting on my behalf. You know all that I desire. You want to deliver the goods!

Please, Lord, help me step aside and not get in the way. Your plan for me is a glorious life. Let me let You lead me to my destiny. Help my mind take a backseat to my heart so that I will be open to our life together.

Oh, Creator of the world, how can I doubt You can create my life? Lead, and let me follow. Indeed, teach me to ride the wave instead of trying to control the ocean.

Affirmations

I pray to make my desires clear to me.

I step aside and allow the Creator to deliver that which I desire.

Reflection

Oh, why can't we let go? We want something so much, we have to beat it down harder and harder until we nearly kill it, don't we? Let it go. Think of that one thing that you desire that you have to have in order to be whole.

Now, what if you never get that thing? Come to terms with that right now. Suppose you never get that thing and find out on your deathbed. You will think, *Oh, how disappointed I am with myself for having this one thing rule my waking thoughts!* Drop it. Let your desire be simply to be a giver and recipient of love. Take this new desire out of your head, and tuck it inside your heart.

Say good-bye to that thing that you feel you have to have or you will not be a perfect human being. Because I can tell you this: God knows you are a perfect human being. Now, are you saying you don't agree with this viewpoint? How silly does that sound? Say good-bye to the incessant desire ruling your thoughts. Ask God to replace it with acceptance and a greater love for yourself and others.

My Reflections

_____

_____

_____

_____

_____

_____

_____

_____

_____

_____

_____

_____

_____

_____

_____

_____

_____

Day 5
Evening Message

Talk to God. He/She/Universe/Source/All-That-Is wants to hear from you.

Imagine for a moment how large and loving our Creator is. He/She knows you individually as well as He/She knows me. What a force that is! How glorious to imagine, if we can!

Here's the thing: God wants us, little human us, to start thinking like Him/Her. That means to start loving like Him/Her. Say yes more than you say no. How used to saying no we have become. Let go of "no" and say "yes" to opportunity. We are so used to shutting it off. The next time somebody asks you to do something, think before saying no. Maybe this is a yes in the making.

Prayer

Dear Lord, thank You. Thank You for bringing this book through me. Thank You for hearing me when I said, "Yes, I will do this." I am grateful for Your love, and I am grateful that I can express it through this book.

Lord, what's next for this reader? How will You speak through me? Will I say yes the first time You ask, or will I need more persuasion?

Lord, help me hear Your call and help me express You to others so that we may live and reign forever with You. Amen.

Affirmations

Lord, I open myself up to saying yes to Your love and expressing it to others.

I am open to opportunities that I previously did not consider.

Reflection

Pat yourself on the back; give yourself a cheer! You have been through a mind-meld. You have melded your mind with the Big Heart of our Creator. What is He/She teaching us to do? Only to be more present and loving with ourselves and others.

He/She tells us He/She is there if we need help. And we do. We cannot go it alone. Without Him/Her, we are runners who cannot walk, dancers who cannot move, and singers with no voices. We need our Creator to make us whole. We need our Creator to complete us, to guide us, and to inspire us.

Take a moment, more if you can, to reflect on the glory of God in the highest. How magnificent is His/Her love, and how gracious a partner He/She is. How strong we are together. Remember He/She is always there. Sometimes, we need to raise our vibration to be in our highest expression of His/Her love. Let's vow to return to our highest love together.

My Reflections

_____

_____

_____

_____

_____

_____

_____

_____

_____

_____

_____

_____

_____

_____

_____

_____

_____

PART IV

THREE SIMPLE STEPS TO CHANGING YOUR LIFE: A NEW METHOD TO HELP PEOPLE STUCK IN A RUT, A DEPRESSION, OR JUST A BAD HABIT

The last bit of inspiration I'll share in this book for spiritual guidance is a special segment on an easy way to change your life now. It's called: "Three Simple Steps to Changing Your Life: A New Method to Help People Stuck in a Rut, a Depression, or Just a Bad Habit."

It's a bit personal, but so is each of our individual relationships with God. God meets us where we are and communicates on our level based on our experience. This is a one-on-one experience that I thought would be helpful to others. It's interesting to me how closely it resembles the law of attraction. I know that law to be a three-step practice based on the Teachings of Abraham through Esther and Jerry Hicks: First, you ask. Second, Source gives. Third, we open ourselves to receive.

There are just three steps to this method. They are:

Step 1: You must ask for help or healing energy.

Step 2: You must allow the help/healing energy to come to you.

Step 3: Follow the direction, guidance, or the energy that is presented.

I'll explain each step briefly using examples from my own life.

Step 1: You must ask for help or specific healing energy.

In order to be in step 1, you really have to be fed up. The problem must really come to a head, like the need for a root canal. Or you must really want to change something, if not everything, about your life. The reason I say everything is because one small change will affect your whole life. Let me explain with an example.

In March of 2010, I found myself in a tailspin of coffee-drinking, candy-eating, driving everywhere (no walking), and sleeping at home every chance I got. This binge set me down a course where I had little energy to clean my house and make fresh meals for my family, two things that used to make me feel good. At the time, I also didn't treat my teenage boys with respect. I found myself barking orders at them more than opening up to them at a time when it was crucial to have open communication and affection.

So there I was: hating my actions and watching my husband pick up the slack. In addition to the laundry, he'd cook sometimes and clean the kitchen most times. This was often after he had put in ten-hour workdays.

In fairness to me, I was also starting my business and doing a lot of computer work putting out a new children's book and marketing the book and my new services. I was also working part-time two to three days a week as a TV newswriter. Now that I am writing this, I see that I was not the total slug I felt I was. I see now that I needed the rest I was taking, but it certainly didn't feel justified to me. And I certainly could have treated the boys with more love. In addition, the sugar from the candy I was eating wasn't helping me, nor was the poor diet I was hooked on. In short, I wanted more energy to complete more tasks more enjoyably. Even if I did need the rest I was taking, I also needed to exercise and eat well. And I wasn't doing either. So I asked God for help. Very simply, this is what I said:

"Lord, please give me the strength to exercise, cook fresh meals for my family, and stop eating the leftover Easter candy."

Asking God for help is one of the easiest things to do once you decide to do it. So decide to ask God for help.

Step 2: You must allow the healing energy to come to you. That means releasing fear and other things you cling to that prevent you from opening up.

After you ask for direction or guidance or help from God, it will come. That's assured. Some who feel energy will feel it in their aura. I'll give you an example. On April 8, 2010, I felt a ball of energy just above my forehead. I now know this is an extension of my third eye energy. At that time, I typically felt guidance coming into the crown of my head. But this feeling was different. Your guidance may or may not come this way. But if you can feel energy, you will know where it is and where it is going. For two days, this block or ball of energy hovered above my forehead at about a forty-five-degree angle outward. I lived with it and waited for its or my next move.

At about midnight April 8, I spoke to it. I said, "Energy, if you are here to help me with my addictions, please come in." But I didn't have total confidence about the new energy. To tell you the truth, I was afraid. So I put up barriers to protect myself. I said, "Energy, you are allowed in, if you serve the light and you are helping me for the greater good."

You don't always have to protect yourself when it comes to healing energy; you can have total trust that only the greater good is around you at all times. But for me, even after seven years of working with God energy directly, I still feared the power of evil. So I protect myself with my thoughts and prayers. By prayers, I mean petitions rather than ritualized words—although I use them too when I can't form my own words for whatever reason.

So you must release fear and ask the energy to come into you. Allow it to enter your body, physically or ethereally (keeping it in your aura, which surrounds your body). Either way, it will be there to help you.

In my case, I felt the energy going into my head, but only partially. Remember, I had stipulations, so I felt half the energy coming in, in pieces, and the other half still floating around me. By the morning of April 10, I was telling the energy if it was here to help me, I was inviting all of it to come in.

It wasn't until I had a good night's rest that I was comfortable inviting all the energy in. (As a general rule, in the morning, we feel more open. At night, it's usually the time we feel most fearful.) The fear I felt the night before, I believe, kept me from receiving all the desired energy that was available to me. In the light of day, I am more open to receiving. You probably are as well. So I did take it all in.

Step 3: Take Action. Now. It's time to do it.

On this morning, I woke up and did a sun salutation (a salute to the sun in yoga poses) before waking my son up to drive him downtown for his advanced algebra class. It is a privilege for him to take this high-school class while still in the eighth grade, but it is an added responsibility on my schedule. It was an extra drive into the city, which actually could cause a lot of stress in my life as it was then. In earlier days, an extra drive into the city would be something to sneeze at, not a big deal in other words. But being in a physical and mental rut, I was looking at the drive as a burden more times than I'd like. On this morning, the yoga gave me something to help me change my attitude.

Sometimes taking action means doing yoga or taking a walk. Sometimes, it means changing a thought and replacing a negative with a positive one. If I think about how much I love my fourteen-year-old son and how much I enjoy his company, I can eventually turn my thought of a burden to drive downtown to *Oh, what a pleasure it will be. I get to have my son all to myself for an hour.* And while we're in traffic, I'll find out where he stands in his fantasy baseball league. I'll quiz him on his Battle of the Books notes, and I'll find myself glancing over at him to see his beautiful, innocent, and pure expressions of excitement, worry, and relaxation—all in one car ride. It will be an adventurous trip, and I will be with a beautiful human being, one who makes me laugh and makes me proud all in the same moment, now.

An added note about *now.*

Now is the only time we can make a change—not Monday morning or some future date. Now we can decide to change a behavior. Start paving the way. Decide that you want to change a behavior that you no longer feel good about. Make a small change in your life, and see how greatly your life changes.

But sometimes we don't know what is keeping us from making a change.

Emotional issues could be keeping you in your rut or even depression. Address the emotional issue that is of most concern. Dig for it, because it might not be evident at first. After all, we hide them because we don't want to face them. For some reason, we think they are too powerful. But in reality, it's the evading of the issue that is slowly killing us with perhaps a poor diet or abuse of alcohol or any other action that does not honor our authentic self.

I will give an example here and share my issue with the burden of carrying our financial debt. The responsibility was eating me up. I needed to get this out on the table and look at it with my husband. A little background: a disability from work led me to rely on credit cards for shopping as well as my son's tuition payments. There was a time when I wrote checks for things with no thought about how I would pay for them, because I was making income to support the spending. But now we were living a different story and I could not continue to carry this burden because I was not working full-time. I kept justifying the spending, because I thought I would go back to working full-time and I would eventually catch up with the credit. But weeks turned into months until I woke up one day and I had been out of work for a year. My credit debt was in the tens of thousands. For a year after that, I tried to manage it, but it all got the best of me. I had to bring my husband into the discussion about how the burden of these payments could be lifted from my shoulders.

Acknowledging my inability to manage the credit cards brought up the feeling of shame. My mind admonished me for getting into such a predicament. It also brought up fear. What would my husband think if he knew I couldn't manage the credit cards? Isn't it interesting how sometimes our minds keep us from getting the help we need? It seems as if our minds would like to stay in an old story that is no longer relevant instead of changing with the times.

Sometimes, our minds keep us from seeing answers to our problems. In times of trouble or even in ordinary times, we should occasionally put our mind in the backseat. Just stop thinking about consequences, and ask questions more. When we ask questions, it refocuses our minds from knowing all to being in the wonder of it all. In my credit card case, I asked my husband how he could help me lift the pressure of managing the payments.

Action, step 3, is the hardest part because that's the one where we have to move our body, change a thought, or ask a question. But make the first move and the second one is easier; then the third step will seem even easier. You may experience setbacks, but you will be on the right track to changing your behavior. And eventually, the new you will take hold.

A final word about experiencing setbacks:

We all experience setbacks. But put a clock on it. Allow your setback one day or one week. But then start with step 1 again. Ask God for help. Replenish your energy with lots of rest, and above all, love yourself. Congratulate yourself for all you do. Don't focus on the one or two things you'd like to do better. Ask for help, and then let it go. Enjoy yourself, enjoy your life, and appreciate all the good that is there in spite of the one or two things you'd like to change.

Now, you've decided to change this (fill in the blank). Move on to more things in your life that make you smile. For me, it is my children, the fresh air in the room, and the budding trees with this spring season. With these three things, my life is full and free for love. That's my focus today.

I couldn't leave without a few thank yous.

Thank you to Louise Hay and Hay House Radio. Thank you to all Hay House authors. Some of your work I know in my heart, all of your work I know by sight.

Thank you to one of the earliest editors of Forty Days and Forty Nights with Spirit, Donna Benedetto Thomsen and her husband and my friend, Brian Thomsen.

Thank you to all the Balboa Press editors and Brandon Grew who coordinated my project.

Thank you to Goran Coban and Adam Rivera of Goran Coban Salon in Chicago. Goran you inspire me with your love of beauty and your generosity; Adam with your creativity. Thank you Karen Kring for your inspirations and photography during my photo shoots. And thank you JT Donchak for your help as an assistant, and son, and friend.

Thank you to my employers and coworkers for accepting me in spite of my own doubts.

Thank you to my extended family of aunts, uncles and cousins who are always kind and open, and who have taught me a lot about how to live, love and laugh.

Thank you to my Spiritual family here in the physical and in the nonphysical. Without my spiritual family in the nonphysical this book would not be in your hands. And thank you to my spiritual peeps on Facebook and in the neighborhood. You are always open to sharing your thoughts and challenging my beliefs and helping me grow.

Thank you to my in-laws, Pete and Pearl Donchak, for being there for me and my family through the years. Thank you Pete for keeping in touch even though you are no longer with us physically.

Thank you to my mother, father, brothers and sisters. You helped me create who I am. I'm happy and honored to have a front row seat as you grow into who you're becoming. Love sharing this time/space with you all.

Finally, thank you to my husband John and my sons John Thomas and Andrew. You guys allow me to be who I am without apology. Thanks for taking the journey with me.

Thank you, thank you, thank you. I am blessed.
Namaste

Other Joy Media Titles:

The Essence Inspired I Am Beautiful Journal
by Geri Hearne, Graciela Zozaya, and The Essence
Journal
This twenty-one-day journal helps you go from blah to beautiful!
It's designed bring you to the place of love. It documents a three-week
process suggested by interdimensional teachers, The Essence of All. Geri
also shares her experience with the process.
ISBN # 978-0-9800954-4-9

The Joy Journal
by Geri Hearne
Journal
This twenty-one-day journal helps you find your joy.
Source tells you how important you are to your soul, how important your
soul is to God, and how very important God is to you.
ISBN # 978-0-9800954-5-6

Poems for Benjamin: A New Mother's Journey
by Rose Hester-Lavenburg
A charming book of poetry inspired by Rose's son Benjamin and husband,
Erik. It offers a no-holds-barred look at the details of the first three years
of Benjamin's precious life. We like to say it's good, bad, and drippy.
But in truth, it's all good! Rose puts pen to paper and describes the new
responsibilities and the confusion, and she even battles postpartum
depression. Rose is a working woman who is just learning her new role
as working mom.
ISBN # 978-0-9800954-3-2

The Dance
DVD created by Sydney Lok
The Dance is a moving meditation inspired by the Spanish Peaks of
Wahatoya in Colorado. It is an ancient, core yoga movement of spiritual
fitness for everyone! Dance and then download; move and then journal.

The Dance will move the energy in your body to show you the blocks preventing you from being the best you!

ISBN # 978-0-9800954-0-1

Just Me and the Trees

Book + CD by Julia Cohn

Illustrated by Gerarda Connolly

Author Julia Cohn is a yoga instructor and is versed in ayurveda and holistic nutrition. She is also a mom. Julia uses her journalistic training to introduce meditation to children ages three through eight.

Illustrator Gerarda Connolly offers her magical crayon to inspire this book to come alive. It's a charming way to offer both parents and children a delightful time-out!

ISBN # 978-0-9800954-1-8

In loving memory

My mom, Ann Hearne, passed away on Mother's Day weekend in 2014. As I make the final edit on this book only one month later, I can feel her loving presence with me. She, along with my dad, who passed in 1991, have given me the strength to be myself. I miss you both and am grateful for your everlasting presence in my life.

Thank you.